E N

ICULT

LATIVES

HAPPEN

TO GOOD

PEOPLE

*Surviving your family and
keeping your sanity*

Dr LEONARD FELDER

D0319119

...shed in the UK in 2004 by
R... ...onal Ltd
7–1... ...dos Street
London
W1G 9AD
www.rodale.co.uk

Printed and bound in the UK by CPI Bath using acid-free paper from sustainable sources
1 3 5 7 9 8 6 4 2

Book design by Joanna Williams

A CIP record for this book is available from the British Library
ISBN 1-4050-6729-2

This paperback edition distributed to the book trade by Pan Macmillan Ltd

Notice
This book is intended as a reference volume only, not as a medical manual. The information given here is designed to help you make informed decisions about your health. It is not intended as a substitute for any treatment that may have been prescribed by your doctor. If you suspect that you have a medical problem, we urge you to seek competent medical help. Also, reading about family conflicts can be stressful for some people. If you have been diagnosed with a serious mental illness, or if you have ever been prescribed medication for a psychiatric condition, or if you are feeling agitated while thinking about this topic, it is recommended that you consult a qualified physician or mental health professional before reading or using any of the suggestions in this book.

The names and identifying details in the case histories in this book have been changed to protect confidentiality.

To my amazing sister, Janice.

Even though we are different from each other,

the love and closeness will last forever.

ACKNOWLEDGEMENTS

This book has been blessed with the contributions of many caring and supportive people. My agent Andrew Stuart guided it wisely from the start. The staff at Rodale has been helpful in so many ways: Stephanie Tade, Amy Rhodes, Troy Juliar, Chris Potash, Cathy Gruhn, Mary Lengle, Dana Bacher, Leslie Schneider, Kelly Schmidt, Jackie Dornblaser and numerous others worked hard to make this project a success.

Additional insights and help were offered by good friends Teri Bernstein, Peter and Carol Reiss, Marc Sirinsky and Catherine Coulson, Trudi Alexy, Deborah Bronner, Sandra Kaler, Laura Pawlowski, Miriam Raviv, Beth Rosenberg, Harriet Shapiro, Anita Siegman and Barbara Zheutlin. I am also grateful to the men and women who taught me over the years to write and do psychological research – James Michael, Sean Austin and Rowland Shepard at Kenyon College, Tom Bonoma at the University of Pittsburgh, Harold Bloomfield and Adelaide Bry in San Diego.

Several members of my own family have been enormously loving and supportive to my work. They include Martin and Ena Felder, Helen Rothenberg Felder, Janice, Craig, and Erica Ruff, Nellie Kolb, Andi Bittker, Ruthe McCabe, Ron Wagner, the Schorin and Wilstein families in Pittsburgh and Los Angeles, the Bayer family in New York and Vermont, and the Felder and Rothenberg families in Michigan and Florida.

I especially want to thank my creative and loving wife and best friend Linda Schorin, as well as our wonderful son Steven, for all the warmth and joy they bring to each day. And I thank God that I have been given the chance to work as a therapist and a writer on a topic as compelling as this.

CONTENTS

INTRODUCTION

Why do difficult relatives happen to good people? I've found that no matter how intelligent or nice you are, there is still a high likelihood that at least one member of your immediate or extended family will hurt you or someone you love. Just flash back to the incidents in recent months and years when a parent, step-parent, in-law, ex-spouse, aunt, uncle, sister, brother, son, daughter or other family member did or said something that made you want to explode.

Now imagine for a moment what your life would be like if you could avoid getting stressed or upset when interacting with these infuriating relatives. What kind of vitality and energy would be freed up if you spent less time arguing and strategizing inside your own head about how – or if – to deal with your difficult relatives? How would it feel if you knew your next family gathering wasn't going to be dominated or ruined by a certain individual because you could handle the situation? *When Difficult Relatives Happen to Good People* will show you how.

A WIDESPREAD PROBLEM

It's been a number of years since I co-authored the best-selling book *Making Peace with Your Parents* and began giving workshops on making peace within your family. Wherever I go, I'm always amazed at the number and variety of people who take me aside to tell me their private stories of dealing with difficult relatives.

Based on a research study I've been conducting, I've found that most people experience significant tension at one or more family events each year, especially at Christmas, Easter, weddings, birthdays, funerals and other rites of passage. Even if there is a geographical buffer between you and your relatives, there is likely to be an underlying discomfort every time you speak on the telephone or inevitably find yourself at a family function face to face with a particular sibling, parent, in-law, grown child or other problem relative.

In terms of actual numbers, I've interviewed a random sample of 1,358 men and women from a range of races, income groups and family configurations. I had expected that maybe 30 to 40 per cent of people would describe their family gatherings as tense or difficult. But to my surprise, I found that 75 per cent of men and women have at least one family member who gets on their nerves, and 68 per cent of us describe family celebrations as either frustrating or an obligation that we don't enjoy. (For the complete results of my polling research, see the appendix on page 239.)

It's clear from this study that there are more people who experience stress than bliss with their extended families. No matter how many magazines you read about setting a lovely table or preparing the perfect meal, the problem still remains: how do you keep difficult relatives from ruining your chance to celebrate with the irreplaceable people in your extended family who won't be around forever?

'I DON'T KNOW HOW I WILL SURVIVE MY HUSBAND'S FAMILY'

Each of us has a unique family, yet there are certain personality types and typical conflicts that arise in thousands of families. Do any of the following sound familiar?

Elaine has a very opinionated mother-in-law. In fact, I remember one session in which Elaine told me her mother-in-law was keeping a notebook of the things Elaine was doing wrong. 'My husband saw the notebook sitting on my mother-in-law's kitchen table. It was filled with things she doesn't like about how I dress, how I don't keep the house clean enough, and how I'm not doing things right for her son and her grandchildren. I don't know how I'll survive my husband's family.'

Bruce is an excellent school teacher who has won awards for his creative programmes helping inner-city youngsters become successful in life. The one time when Bruce feels like a failure, however, is when he visits his family. 'My dad is a lawyer, my brother is a lawyer and my sister is an investment banker. When I arrive at family dinners, they glance at my ten-year-old car and they give me a look that says, "Poor Bruce, he's such a failure." I sometimes wonder why I keep turning up for these family torture sessions.'

Kirsten is possibly the most amazing social planner you could ever meet. She can arrange enormously interesting dinner parties and create spectacular celebrations for her friends' birthdays. The only Kirsten-arranged events that are likely to fail are when she has her relatives over for a family get-together. 'There just doesn't seem to be a way to bring my relatives together without it turning into a painful mess. My father and his new wife both drink too much and start saying things that suck the air out of the room. My 22-year-old daughter loves to stir up trouble; last Christmas, she turned up with a new boyfriend who could only be described as on hiatus between prison stays. My older brother the doctor is married to an incredible snob who always finds something about me to criticize. I've also got two cousins who can't be seated at the same table because they fell out in business with each other and the bitterness flares up whenever they're together. Next year I think we should all go to McDonald's and order Happy Meals.'

If you're being honest, the chances are you can relate to at least one of these situations, or to a similar story involving your own family but with its own maddening twist.

WHAT CAN BE DONE?

If there's someone in your family that you don't get along with – or, perhaps they don't get along with you – then do something about it. For instance, if there is a specific family member whose sole purpose in life seems to be to push your buttons, let's find a way to reduce the impact this person has on you. Or if there is a family event that you dread attending because you know there's going to be tension, let's work on a way to make this event less stressful and more fulfilling. Or if you find yourself trying so hard to juggle the needs of *all* your difficult relatives that you're at your wit's end, let's remedy the situation.

In this book, you will find easy-to-follow, practical steps you can take in order to:

- Understand more deeply what causes the tensions in your particular family;

- Sort out which relatives you can get closer to and which ones to keep at a distance;

- Identify what makes phone calls and visits so problematic, and what you can do to help improve these basic family interactions;

- Clarify and come to terms with the money, status and competition issues that are causing friction between members of your family;

- Explore and offer creative solutions for the religious conflicts and lifestyle/values clashes that flare up in more families today than ever before;

- Find out why people in your family tend to make hurtful or insensitive comments about each other's weight, appearance or other sensitive subjects – and what you can do to keep family events from turning into a dreadful onslaught of criticism and advice-giving;

- Learn what you can control and what you can't control regarding family members who have addictions to drugs, alcohol, gambling and other problems;

- Heal yourself from past hurts and disappointments in your family, so that you can make sure you break the legacies of pain that can be passed down and damage your own children and your adult romantic partner;

- Learn profound lessons about your own life's journey and personal growth by examining what you want to keep and what you want to discard from your family patterns;

- Find the right words to confront family members who are abusive or hurtful, and avoid approaches that might make matters worse.

When Difficult Relatives Happen to Good People uses humour, true stories and helpful insights to address one of life's most perplexing challenges: how to get on better with even your most difficult relative.

WHAT TO EXPECT

I can't promise that if you read this book your self-centered sister will miraculously become a compassionate human being, or that your wealthy, belligerent uncle will learn humility. But I predict that if you think about and use some of the suggestions I offer, you will become far more skilled at surviving your time with them with your sanity intact.

In addition to the stories and techniques that come from counselling my clients and workshop participants, I will include a few examples from my own family. Both my wife, Linda, and I have several relatives whom we love in our hearts but are quite frankly challenging to deal with.

I remember one particular family dinner when a few aunts and uncles were screaming at each other in a huge argument. These adult siblings who love one another were nevertheless ripping into each other verbally and saying extremely hurtful things. I turned to my wife Linda's 90-year-old grandmother to see if the shouting match was upsetting her. Grandma Ruth, who had a great sense of humour, looked around and then looked back at me as she said calmly, 'Isn't it great to have the family together again?'

On another occasion, my wife and I were driving home from an especially stressful family event. We were exhausted from all the tension of the evening. There was a long silence in the car. Then, out of nowhere, Linda said in an ironic tone of voice, 'It's all relatives.' We both started laughing.

I mention these two stories because I want you to know how important humour, a sense of irony and a positive perspective can be in dealing with even extremely serious and painful family issues.

One of the key themes of this book is that even if you can't change your relatives, you can significantly change and improve how you respond to them. In each of the chapters that follows, you will learn how to stop falling into the same traps and battles that have frustrated you in the past. You will discover creative ways to transform your family get-togethers, even if your difficult relative continues to exhibit the same personality traits that used to ruin each interaction. In addition, this book will give you personal insight that can help you feel a lot less victimized and a lot more comfortable with your family.

I strongly believe, and have seen repeatedly, that our family interactions are like a crucible where we get tested and shaped by heated emotions and fiery disputes. In a meaningful way, your family difficulties will force you to work out who you really are – or else your relatives will dictate who they expect you to be.

Over the years I've counselled many terrific people who've felt that their personalities were being trampled on by certain relatives. My hope is that this book will help you or someone you love find solid ways to be protected against such hurt. I also will be suggesting numerous ways in which your spirit may become stronger and more alive as a result of these encounters with your relatives. My intention is that this book will not only improve the quality of your family gatherings, but also transform the way you feel inside when you are face to face with your most difficult relatives.

CHAPTER ONE

WHY DO CERTAIN RELATIVES UPSET YOU AT SUCH A DEEP LEVEL?

Let's face it – there are times when family members do hurtful, selfish, insensitive, obnoxious things. It might be a father or father-in-law who can't stop offering unsolicited advice and criticism, or a mother or mother-in-law who tries to make you feel guilty for having a life of your own. It could be a step-parent or step-child who feels threatened by you and does things to make your life miserable. It might be a sister or brother who receives preferential treatment, or who has never stopped competing with you. Maybe it's a grown-up daughter or son – or grandchild – who frustrates you with his or her unreliability. It might be a member of the family who is terribly judgmental about your personal life, or one who tries to shove religious or political beliefs down your throat.

As a psychologist, the first thing I do is check with the person sitting in front of me to gauge if the family issue bothering him or her feels like a tiny irritation or a significant upset. Does the relative strongly get on your nerves or is the person easy to ignore? It would be wrong for a therapist to rush into an assumption that some family incident has deep meaning when it doesn't. Despite what Freud may have said a hundred years ago, sometimes a cigar is just a cigar – and sometimes a complaint about an obnoxious family member is just a minor speed hump on the highway of life.

But for most of us there are, from time to time, hurtful family interactions that hit us especially hard and need to be addressed. There are certain confrontations that stick in your mind and undermine your sense of well-being with surprising ferocity. You may have said to yourself, 'Oh, I'm just going to ignore so-and-so. He's done this crap before and he'll probably do it again.' But something in your head or your gut just won't let it go this time. Something about this person's insensitivity is gnawing at your insides and you need to discover what it is so you can regain your peace of mind and your optimum effectiveness.

Think back on your recent family get-togethers. Are there some family members who can mouth off and be rude to you and you can shrug it off or ignore it, while other relatives get under your skin and make you want to scream at the slightest comment? Who are these relatives that make you want to lash out in anger? What are the incidents that still make your blood boil when you think about them? It's important to identify who's who, because if you try to gloss over your strong emotional upset regarding certain relatives you will only make matters worse. Pretending you are fine when you are actually seething inside only causes the unexplored hurt feelings to take hold of you even more strongly.

Based on what I've learned from my clients and workshop participants over the past twenty years, there are two basic ways of understanding why certain relatives and certain incidents upset you on a deep level. As you think about the frustrations you have in your own family, ask yourself which of the following explanations rings most true for you.

YOU MIGHT BE EMBARRASSED

When your own flesh and blood says or does something offensive or cruel, it's got to make you wonder, 'Am I really related to this person? How is that possible?' For example, you may be shocked when your own brother insults a guest you've brought to dinner. Or you might feel the sting of resentment when your spoiled cousin or opinionated aunt comments that you'd look great if only you'd lose ten pounds. Or maybe you're humiliated when your child plays up in public and you feel the glare of onlookers as they say under their breath, 'Doesn't that parent know how to control her child?' Or you might be mortified when your parents or in-laws say the most embarrassing things in front of someone you had hoped to impress.

I've found that a common reason people get angry and hurt by the obnoxious behaviour of their family members is because they believe that the misbehaviour or abrasive personality of their relative is a direct reflection on them. Particularly if you are a caring and sensitive person, you might think, 'I'm not safe being seen in public with this relative,' or 'I'll never be able to show my face again if people know I'm related to this person who's so inappropriate.' It may feel as if your most obnoxious relative is announcing to the world, 'This is who we really are! We have absolutely no class and don't let anyone fool you into thinking otherwise!' It's as if you are holding your breath, hoping no one will notice that you come from the same gene pool.

Relatives are strange by design

If you stop for a moment and look at the situation from a scientific perspective, it makes perfect sense that you are not responsible and should not feel embarrassed about the sometimes-strange behaviour that goes on in your family. In fact, from a scientific perspective it is obvious that in every family there tends to be at least one individual who is troubled, unpleasant, insensitive or worse.

In the past ten years there have been some exciting discoveries by the scientists conducting the human genome project in which our personality traits and other genetic predispositions are being mapped according to the chromosomes, enzymes and biochemical variations that strongly influence how we look and behave. One of the remarkable findings has been that there seems to be, *by design*, a range and severity of personality diversity among members of the same family. Parents who have more than one child know this to be true – from early infancy each child has a distinct and unique personality. Just because relatives may be alike in many of their physical and other features, their personalities can still be quite different.

What's especially revealing in the human genome research is that *within every family there tends to be a full range of individual variations on a particular personality trait.* Let's take for instance a personality factor such as self-absorbed behaviour. You know what a narcissist is: in the Greek myth, Narcissus only wanted to look at his own reflection. It's the member of your family who loves talking about himself, who thinks the world revolves around him. It's the person in your family who feels entitled to special treatment or who always wants things her own way. It's the family member who might do something nice for you but only if it flatters his self-image in the long run.

Genetic research shows that in families there are usually one or two people who are prone to narcissistic tendencies. These 'huge dose' individuals tend to be charming but arrogant, driven, inflexible and unable to have empathy for the needs and feelings of others.

In this same family you might have one or two others who were born with a medium dose of the biochemistry that favours narcissism. These 'medium dose' individuals have selfish moments but can be empathetic at times. They are ambitious but capable of considering the needs and feelings of others as well. They have far less self-absorption than the flaming narcissists in the family, but enough drive and self-worth to be successful in the world.

Finally, in this same family there is often a third type of person who received a significantly lower dose of the genes, chromosomes and enzymes that lead to narcissism. This third type of family member might have a painfully low level of self-centredness and a huge helping of empathy and flexibility. This extra-nice individual sometimes gets used as a sounding board or even at times treated like a doormat by the more narcissistic members of the family.

In most families, people tend to judge and criticize one another for exhibiting different levels of a particular personality trait. The highly self-absorbed/narcissistic family member might be thinking or saying, 'I wish my other family members weren't such weaklings and failures.' At the same time, the less narcissistic family members might be thinking or saying, 'I wish my other family members weren't so obnoxiously self-centred and demanding.' In most cases, the various family members feel upset and offended at the idea that someone from their own family is so different from what he or she thinks is the right way to be. Rather than accepting that each family is genetically designed to exhibit a diversity of personality traits, we spend a lot of time and energy feeling horrified, hurt or angry that our relatives are so unlike us.

What if you were to embrace the diversity in your family and say to yourself, 'What an amazing collection of different characters we are. What an odd combination of seemingly incompatible personalities we were born with in this family. Hooray!' What if instead of resisting the mysterious spiritual and biological design of the universe, you could simply take a breath and say, 'Astonishing. Our family gene pool manages to contain both an insensitive bully and a real softie!'

I'm not saying you have to bury your head in the sand and give up completely on trying to help or influence your loved ones. If a member of your family is trying to change and asks you for help, you should feel free to help him in whatever way you can. If an impulsive or insensitive family member needs someone to set a firm limit for her so that she won't trample on the feelings and needs of others, then by all means do. And, if a family member's hurtful habits or mental illness are severe enough, try your best to be a positive influence. Point him in the direction of his family doctor, a good therapist or an inspiring mentor, but don't feel responsible for his inappropriate behaviour. As Reinhold Niebuhr said so eloquently almost eighty years ago, 'Please grant me the serenity to accept the things I cannot change, to change those things I can change, and to recognize the difference.' (See Chapters Two and Three for more on setting healthy limits with difficult relatives.)

One of the best ways to break free of the pain of having a difficult relative is to remind yourself – often! – not to feel guilty, shocked or offended by what is beyond your control. Even though you may be related to this person, you are not able to control his thoughts, actions or words. Or at least I hope you don't have that job – it would be so time-consuming and exhausting to try to run someone else's life.

Using humour to break free of your usual reaction

What can you do during a tense moment to break the habit of becoming upset, furious or embarrassed because of the misbehaviour of a difficult relative? The next time you are in a public place with a parent, child, in-law or other relative who does something that normally would make you want to cringe or explode, try saying to yourself, with ironic humour, 'I bet everyone thinks I am related to this person. Hah! What they don't know is that I have never ever met this person and I haven't a clue why anyone would think otherwise.' Or you can take some of the sting out of the situation by saying calmly to yourself, 'I wonder whose relative that person is?' and just smile inside for a moment. Or you can say to yourself, 'If I were somehow in control of my relative's personality or behaviour, I definitely could feel upset right now. But since I'm not in charge of her life, I can just watch her with the detachment of an anthropologist from Sweden who would find this person fascinating, a bit bizarre, and probably worthy of an entire dissertation.'

This technique might not work every time, and there still may be incidents that absolutely get under your skin. But if you practise detaching yourself, or your emotional well-being, from the other person's behaviour, you will gradually see some progress. You are likely to find that you become much less disgruntled by even your most difficult relative's nonsense. You will find that you can save yourself a lot of aggravation by looking at your family member with a compassionate calmness as you say, 'We are different people – always have been and always will be.'

**'I wonder whose daughter
that unpleasant girl could be?'**

To illustrate the practicality of dry humour and detachment, consider my client Beatrice, who is a phenomenal parent (most of the time) but who happens to have an extremely volatile and confrontational teenage daughter called Jenna, who pushes Beatrice beyond her limit every so often. After numerous incidents where Jenna's verbal insults and stubbornness caused Beatrice to question why she ever became a parent, Beatrice came for counselling.

She told me, 'I feel like I'm a complete failure with my daughter. Sometimes Jenna upsets me so much that I start yelling back at her and I become almost as out of control as she is. I feel as though Jenna is determined to humiliate me in public, and I can't seem to separate the fact that she's a hormonal teenager and I'm supposed to be the sensible adult.'

To help Beatrice regain her inner strength and her ability to be effective with a troubled teenager who needs an extremely resourceful, firm and loving parent, I urged Beatrice to try the detachment technique described above. We practised a few responses, and Beatrice was ready the next time Jenna pushed her close to the edge.

A perfect opportunity to try out the new technique occurred while out shopping a few days later. Jenna and Beatrice were looking for a new outfit Jenna could wear to a party that was coming up in two weeks. The search for the right dress was going well until Jenna pulled one of her stunts – trying to humiliate her mother in public. Jenna walked up to a stylishly dressed middle-aged sales assistant and said, within Beatrice's earshot, 'Can I tell you that you look great in that outfit? My mother would look awful if she tried to dress like that, but you look incredible.'

Beatrice calmly took a breath and said silently to herself, 'I wonder whose daughter that unpleasant girl could be?' With a sense of inner strength she hadn't felt in a long time, Beatrice knew at that moment she had begun to break free of her old habit of taking it personally and getting excessively upset as a result of Jenna's provocative comments.

Beatrice then said calmly to her daughter, 'I'm so sorry our shopping trip has ended for today. We'll have another chance next week.'

Jenna replied, 'God, Mum, I didn't do anything.'

Beatrice still felt calm and in control as she said gently but firmly, 'I'm your Mum and I'm in charge of making sure you don't say hurtful things to people you care about. So let's go and we'll try again next week because I *do* want to get you the outfit we talked about.'

Jenna snapped back, 'No chance. I want to get it now!'

Beatrice calmly repeated to herself the humour line we had practised, 'I wonder whose daughter that unpleasant girl could be?' Then she firmly but softly whispered to Jenna, 'If you make a scene or if you don't leave right now, we won't be going shopping next week either. It's your choice, Jenna, and for your sake I hope you make the right one.'

Jenna was stunned. Her mother had never been so calm and so resolved when taking away a privilege. Knowing that Beatrice was fully in charge, Jenna silently followed her out of the shop and back into the car. Like hundreds of other clients who have tried these techniques, Beatrice had used silent humour and calm detachment to regain her power and clarity with a highly demanding family member.

**'I don't know if we've met
that strange old man'**

Brian and Katrina used a similar but much less confrontational humour/detachment technique with Brian's divorced father, Walter. For years Brian and Katrina had felt humiliated and resentful at Walter's rudeness and pushiness in public places, especially when they took him to restaurants, where Walter usually felt compelled to boss the staff around. Walter is an intense, self-made entrepreneur who always feels he has to be in control. As he himself put it, 'You have to let people know who's boss or they'll walk all over you.'

Brian and Katrina had planned to take Walter out to a restaurant for his birthday, but they were worried that this dinner would be like dozens of others that had gone badly. Their concerns proved to be well founded when, as soon as they got to the restaurant Walter started bossing around the parking attendant and the wine waiter. He also kept sending the waiters back for all sorts of things throughout the meal.

Brian recalled, 'In the past, this birthday dinner would have been a disaster. I would have shut down emotionally with knots in my stomach. Katrina would have been upset because she would feel unable to let the staff know that we don't agree with my Dad's disrespectful way of treating people. We both would have felt victimized and humiliated, which is an extra price to pay on top of the huge bill we would be paying to treat my dear old Dad on his birthday.'

But this year was different. Brian and Katrina had participated a few weeks earlier in a workshop I'd given on dealing with difficult relatives where they had learned the humour/detachment technique. Their goal was not to get into a power struggle with Walter or attempt to change his underlying personality. Rather, their intention was simply to get through the birthday dinner without feeling humiliated. And, possibly, to enjoy some quality moments of connecting with Brian's father, despite his imperfections.

Katrina explained, 'When my father-in-law started doing his usual number on the restaurant staff, I whispered calmly to Brian, "I don't know if we've met this strange old man." It snapped both of us out of feeling tense or embarrassed. For the first time in years we each felt calm and in charge, even though Walter was doing what used to drive us up the wall. Brian gave an extra-large tip and a personal apology to each of the mistreated employees. Since I wasn't preoccupied with judging or trying to change my father-in-law, I actually enjoyed Walter's stories and his colourful personality. Knowing that he wasn't going to be able to embarrass us this time helped us dodge the uncomfortable moments and focus instead on the fact that he can also be a loving, affectionate and complicated human being.'

Again, the goal is not to change your family member's personality, which in most cases you are powerless to do. But if you significantly change your own reaction to this person, you will find it much easier to notice his good qualities and not just focus on his difficult traits. You will be able to spend time with your most difficult family member and come away feeling a positive connection, even if he's his same old self.

There's a Yiddish expression that goes, 'If you're waiting for your relatives to change … you should live so long.' My suggestion is that instead of holding your breath and saying, 'I won't be happy until this person changes,' you can be much more effective if you focus instead on how to remain healthy yourself. Using humour and detachment helps you regain your sense of maturity and calmness, which are crucial tools for getting through any family gathering successfully.

YOU MIGHT SEE A HIDDEN PART OF YOURSELF

Sometimes the reason we get so upset with our relatives is because we know deep inside that we might be, or we might have been at one time, a little bit like they are. For example, one of your relatives might be a problem drinker or cigarette smoker and you might be a passionate ex-drinker or ex-smoker who can't tolerate being around someone who reminds you of how you once were. Or one of your relatives might be extremely tight with money – some would say mean – and you don't like the part of yourself that is or once was extremely frugal.

Or if one of your relatives has a weight problem and you have spent a lot of time and energy trying to hide or overcome your own weight problem, you might feel angry or humiliated when your overweight relative reaches for that extra helping of dessert. Or if you are insecure about your own educational level or social status, then a relative's grammatical errors might make you cringe. Or if a family member has questionable taste in clothes, furnishings or films and you don't want anyone to notice the fact that you come from the same background, then you might notice yourself squirming every time your family member commits a style faux pas.

As a psychotherapist, I find it fascinating and useful whenever I hear a client getting upset or ranting about a family member's imperfections. It is usually the beginning of a wonderful opportunity for growth for the person sitting in front of me. Specifically, if you take a step back and look at each of the times you feel embarrassed or horrified by someone in your family, you may be able to identify the personal issues that make you most self-conscious, self-critical or insecure.

In this way, your family member's disturbing behaviour provides you with a valuable road map of issues you will need to face yourself if you are going to become a more healthy, relaxed and self-accepting person. In fact, making a mental note of the things you can't stand about your relatives gives you a crucial set of clues as to what you may want to improve in yourself.

The 'thank you for being so unpleasant' card

I sometimes advise my clients to write *but not send* an unusual thank-you note to their most obnoxious or insensitive family member, saying something like, 'Dear _____, I am so glad you are part of my life. Because of you, I have seen more clearly than ever how I don't want to treat people. You are a brilliant example of exactly what I don't want to be like. Thank you for being an example that I will carry inside my mind and use for the rest of my life.'

Some clients have enjoyed simply speaking these words aloud in my office, while others have actually written out the 'Thank you for being so unpleasant' card. Whether you say these words to a counsellor or friend, or whether you write them down and then tear up the card, the goal is to help you tap your sense of humour and your sense of clarity about how this difficult relative is an 'inspiration' – of exactly the kind of person you don't want to become. I insist that you *do not* send the card to your relative because that would stir up additional friction.

There is an important second step in this technique of learning about the type of person you would like to be. The second step is to write down on a piece of paper the two divergent sets of qualities you see in this difficult family member who has been getting on your nerves.

Try answering the following questions, perhaps in a notebook.

1. What traits of this relative do I admire and want to emulate?
2. What traits of this relative do I despise and want to avoid in my own life?
3. What kind of changes should I make and what help will I need to ensure that I don't perpetuate in my own life what I have found so offensive in this family member?

Instead of just getting upset at your difficult relatives, this powerful exercise allows you to learn about yourself and become wiser and healthier. It's as though your most frustrating family members hold a secret gift for you – some clues about the struggle to become a far more compassionate, creative and decent person than he or she has been.

'She's just an idiot'
To illustrate this exercise, I'll use the example of a client named Carol, a divorced woman in her thirties who entered therapy because she wanted to find out what was holding her back from having a successful love relationship. If you met Carol, you'd be shocked to find out that she has been without a serious romantic partner for almost nine years. She's attractive, intelligent and extremely considerate to her parents, her friends from work, and her elderly neighbours.

But when I ask Carol about her family background, I see her face flush as she begins to describe her painful estrangement from her younger sister, Patricia, who has been married three times. 'We were very close when we were children, but I have been upset with Patricia for many years. She's just an idiot– she's got the common sense of a hamster.'

I learn that Carol is angry with her younger sister because Patricia 'always throws herself at men. She's caused my parents huge amounts of heartache. And she continues to be extremely unreliable and immature. Every time there's a family gathering and Patricia turns up, late as usual, I feel like taking her aside and screaming at her to grow up.'

In this counselling session with Carol, I have two choices. I can just nod my head in agreement and not ask her to go too deeply into her own issues. Or I can begin to help Carol do some inner work and turn her frustrations and feelings about her younger sister into an opportunity for her own personal growth.

As you can probably guess, I choose to go for the inner work. I ask Carol, 'Would you be interested in finding out whether your strong negative feelings about Patricia might be a clue about some important issues inside you?'

Carol is a little unsure at first. She says, 'What do you mean? I'm just telling you why I can't stand my sister. This has nothing to do with me or my issues.'

I ask Carol to trust me for a moment, and I promise that if the exercise I suggest feels uncomfortable or uninformative, we can move on to something else. She agrees to give it a try, so I give her a pad of paper and ask her to write down her first reactions to these three questions.

1. Is there anything about Patricia that you do like and would want to incorporate into your own life?

2. Is it possible that Patricia's behaviour is upsetting because it reminds you of something that is hidden or unexpressed in your own personality?

3. Is there anything about Patricia that you would be willing to describe in an unusual thank-you note (and

not send) to say how much you have learned from Patricia about the kind of person you do not want to be?

This brings a smile to Carol's face. She quickly writes a scathing thank-you note:

Dear Patricia,

      Thank you for being such a perfect example of the kind of woman I don't want to be. You dress like a tart and you let men treat you like dirt. You make terrible decisions, always in a rush, without thinking through the consequences. You are the high priestess of self-sabotage. Bearing you in mind will help me make sure I don't fall into the traps you've repeatedly fallen into.

Then we discuss Patricia's good qualities – her spontaneity, her love of music and dance, her joie de vivre and her love of animals, especially how well she cares for her three cats and two dogs.

Finally, we consider the second question. For a moment, Carol is silent. Then a tear begins to emerge from one of her eyes and slowly move down her cheek.

Carol takes a minute more to let her thoughts wander and then tells me, 'When I was in high school I was a lot like Patricia. I was fun, creative, full of life. But I got pregnant by accident and after a long, painful process of trying to make the right decision, I had an abortion. And the boy disappeared. Ever since then I've been extremely cautious and guarded in relationships, which is understandable, I suppose. But I've also been very resentful of Patricia and her wild life. It's upsetting just to be near her and see her doing things in such a carefree way. I don't understand it, but I get quite agitated just from hearing her stories or seeing how she behaves.'

Over the next several sessions, Carol and I work to sort through these complex issues and emotions. We do some intensive grief work to explore her feelings regarding the abortion and about being betrayed by the boyfriend. I direct Carol to write a series of thank-you notes to Patricia (that were torn up and never sent) in which Carol pours out her feelings about how much she has learned from witnessing Patricia's mistakes with men.

We also begin to explore the aspects of Carol and Patricia's 'wildness' that are acceptable or unacceptable to Carol now. Knowing all that she knows and having experienced all that she has experienced, Carol is able to sort out calmly what kind of reserve she feels is necessary and what kind of sensuality she now is willing to explore.

This inner work, which was first triggered by Carol's strongly judgmental feelings about her younger sister, became the basis for several breakthroughs in Carol's life. Carol gradually opened up a bit in her relationships with men and began going out on dates more regularly. She also became a lot less judgmental of Patricia, and much closer to her. As Carol explained, 'Patricia is still not that clever when it comes to dealing with men. But I don't feel as agitated about her private business as I once did. Now when Patricia and I get together for a meal or the cinema, or a visit to a museum, we don't try to change each other. We just enjoy being sisters again with a whole lot of closeness and warmth. She still is a bit of an idiot. But she's family and she's taught me a tremendous amount about how to put on make-up, how to change my haircut to bring out my best features and how to accessorize my favourite outfits. We sometimes disagree about things, and we occasionally argue, but we both know that our love for each other is deeper than whatever tensions flare up between us. After years of being enemies, we're just plain old sisters again, and I'm glad she's in my life.'

Carol recently met a man and the relationship looks promising. She's lucky that the man she's fallen in love with is quite self-aware and willing to work at making a relationship successful. He's caring enough to know that Carol has been betrayed before and needs to be treated with honesty and respect.

I can't guarantee that everyone who writes an unsent note saying 'Thank you for being such a horrific example of who I don't want to be' is going to have a reconciliation with his family member or a breakthrough in her personal life. But I do promise that you will gain a lot of wisdom about who you are and what you want to become if you stop judging your family members and start using their imperfections as a clue for your own inner searching.

Why not start today? Whenever you notice yourself getting worked up or self-righteous about the misbehaviour of someone in your family, slow down and ask yourself: what positive traits do I want to pick up from this person? What hidden or unexpressed aspect of my own personality is this person forcing me to look at? What negative traits do I want to avoid?

If you use this technique, you are bound to find yourself reacting a lot less when your relatives misbehave. Instead, you will be able to focus on enjoying this person's company while protecting yourself from his or her frustrating qualities. Rather than spending family gatherings with your stomach knotted up, you *can* rise above the unpleasantness and hopefully enjoy some moments of closeness and warmth.

CHAPTER TWO

WHEN AND HOW TO CHANGE A FAMILY PATTERN YOU DON'T LIKE

Despite your best intentions, when interacting with difficult relatives there's always the chance of things turning ugly. It could be a family gathering where a certain cousin says something designed to rattle you. Or it might be an unpleasant phone conversation with a sibling that descends into harsh words or painful silences. Or it could be just the old familiar guilt dance or power struggle.

At those lovely moments, you may have wondered, 'How did I let myself get drawn in again by this person? Am I a masochist or what?' Now ask yourself this: wouldn't it be great to try something different instead – something that has a chance of changing a family pattern that has been causing you pain for too long?

In Chapter One, the focus was on using detachment and humour to break an old pattern and do some important inner work in response to a difficult family member. This chapter is about confronting the situation more directly. Here you'll learn when might be the right time to speak up or take action, what words and responses can help and which ones tend to make things worse, and what kind of allies to enlist to improve your chances of being successful when you try to break old family patterns that you've disliked for many years.

AVOIDING THE
MOST COMMON MISTAKES

Before working out what approach might work most effectively, it's important to identify what usually doesn't work. Specifically, there are three common responses to family tensions that frequently make things worse. See if you or someone in your family has made the mistake of trying one of the following.

The tell-them-off approach

In the late 1960s and early 1970s, it was fashionable for counsellors to tell their clients to 'release your anger', 'let it all hang out', 'tell them exactly how you feel', and 'show them just how upset you are'. If a client came to a therapy session and said, 'My manipulative sister-in-law has hurt my feelings,' the hip therapist with long, unkempt hair and extra-wide lapels would say, 'You've got to tell her off. You've got to *express your feelings.*'

Those were the days of pounding pillows, primal-scream therapy and hitting one another with rubber-coated bats. It was also a time when people wore paisley shirts and tie-dyed dresses.

We've learned a lot since then. In those days, advocates of 'emotional catharsis' implied that you would feel less resentful, even blissful, after pouring out your anger. But scientific studies have taught us since that offloading on someone doesn't actually reduce the level of anger inside you but rather stirs up feelings of bitterness and revenge in both parties. Research suggests that in most cases, if you have a short fuse it's not likely to get any longer after you have verbally abused the other person.

To break out of the vicious cycle of attacking and counterattacking, watch closely the words you pick and the tone of voice you use. To avoid provoking your most difficult relative into becoming even more defensive or obnoxious, be sure to avoid sweeping accusations such as 'You *always* do this' or 'You *never* do that.' As soon as you say the magic words 'always' or 'never', you can guarantee that your relative will stop listening and start defending himself.

Based on what I have observed in counselling hundreds of families, I would estimate that more than half of all fights happen because someone said the magic words 'You *always*' or 'You *never.*' It's amazing how many conflicts can be avoided or improved just by eliminating those two words from your vocabulary.

The constipated approach

At the other extreme, there's a second mistake that many people make when dealing with their feelings. It happens when you try with all your might not to say or do anything in response to a maddening relative. Have you ever found yourself tightening your jaw and gritting your teeth while a pushy or obnoxious relative fills the room with his or her insensitivity? Have you felt your stomach twisting into knots or your chest tightening while a clique of domineering family members went on and on professing their version of reality? Have you felt helpless and frustrated when a family member was being rude, hurtful or disrespectful?

I call this the constipated approach because that essentially describes what's taking place on a physiological level. This hold-it-all-in response is common among those who consider themselves good, nice or decent. The difficult relative says or does something unpleasant and in response, the 'nice' relative shuts up, holds his or her tongue and feels tense and blocked up inside.

Quite often there are rationalizations that go along with the decision to clam up and do nothing. These include the belief that if you keep silent you are taking the moral high ground and acting more maturely. Or maybe you have reasoned that if you placate or act compliantly toward the rude relative, he or she will eventually come to appreciate you more and treat you better. Fat chance.

If this sounds like you, please don't feel that you are the only one who takes the constipated approach. We all have the tendency to rationalize from time to time.

Most people who clam up when they are around a difficult relative also reason that they have nothing to lose by staying silent. But if you could take an MRI photograph of your jaw, your stomach, your intestines, your shoulders and your heart and lungs at that moment you would see that you are causing quite a bit of internal upset with this constipated approach. Not only are you encouraging the difficult relative to treat you like a doormat, but you are also telling your vital organs, joints and muscles that they are going to have to stay constricted with insufficient oxygen and sluggish bloodflow until some unspecified future time when hell freezes over and your relative miraculously starts to act differently. Don't go on fooling yourself.

The passive-aggressive approach

Finally, there is a third response mode that most of us slip into every so often. Those inclined to use psychological jargon call it passive-aggressive behaviour. In plain English, it's those times when we say to ourselves, 'I won't say anything, I won't say anything, I won't say anything …' and then, on the fourth or fifth or tenth time that your difficult family member hurts your feelings, your anger erupts in an unfortunate manner. The frustration you have been trying to keep locked inside might escape as sarcasm or as a vicious remark you later regret. Or you might start arguing forcefully in an attempt to convince this uncaring family member how wronged you feel, only to find that the relative is likely to respond in turn with defensiveness. You had tried so hard not to let your anger or hurt show and now you find yourself fully engaged after blurting out far more than you intended.

'They worship the ground he walks on'

Carla's case is a good example of how hard it is to respond effectively to a difficult family member. As a sensitive and talented artist who pursues her art part-time while paying the bills by working as a television production assistant, she admits she always felt a bit frustrated with her parents and three siblings, who have been trying to get Carla to stop being an artist and do something 'sensible' like training as an accountant. For years Carla simply tolerated her family get-togethers and tried to avoid family criticism. Carla said, 'I love my family, even with all their conventional opinions and judgments. They're the only family I have, and we used to enjoy some wonderful times in spite of our different lifestyles.'

But eight years ago Carla's older sister Julie married an estate agent, Kevin, who takes great pleasure in poking fun at Carla and telling her how to organize her life. According to Carla, 'There's something about Kevin's hostile jokes and invasive comments that crosses the line. On several occasions Kevin has made fun of my looks, my boyfriends, my bank account and my art to the extent that I've had to walk out of a family gathering so I don't start crying in front of everyone.

My family adores Kevin, probably because he makes a lot of money, but also because he and my sister Julie are the first in the family to produce the precious grandchildren my parents have wanted for a long time. So whenever I tell anyone in the family that Kevin is being hurtful or obnoxious, they look at me as if I'm barmy. "Who cares if he's a little intense sometimes?" they say. "You're just being too sensitive." It takes a lot to reduce me to tears, but on several occasions Kevin has said things that really hit me in a soft spot. I hate that him being able do that to me.'

Like many people who are forced into close contact with a painfully difficult relative every time they turn up for a family event, Carla has attempted several things that haven't worked. She tried at first to tell Kevin off and found he got even more hurtful toward her in response. For a while she tried staying away from family gatherings, but she realized her absence was essentially a victory for Kevin. She then tried being polite and silent, hoping he might stop focusing on her. But this didn't work either, as Kevin always made sure he found the right moment to say something that he knew would rattle Carla. Then Carla began to notice she had become passive-aggressive with him, trying hard to keep her frustration inside but instead stooping to his level every so often with sarcastic and vicious remarks that made her siblings turn to her and say, 'Gosh, Carla, what's getting at you?'

When Carla first came in for counselling, she told me, 'This can't go on. I don't want this creep to ruin every family event for me. But at the moment I dread seeing my family because I hate the way they worship the ground he walks on. I feel as if, should it come to a choice between siding with Kevin or siding with me, they'd definitely side with Kevin.' To help Carla change her approach to this painful situation, I started by focusing on her own sense of self-worth. During our first few sessions I worked with Carla to help her feel stronger about her gifts as an artist and her right to be different from the rest of her family. As Eleanor Roosevelt said, 'No one can make you feel inferior without your consent.'

I asked Carla to make a list of all the people in her life who do appreciate her art, her humour, her kindness, her generosity and her strength as a human being. As with many people who feel like outsiders in their own families, Carla soon understood, 'I'm in trouble if I keep waiting for my family to tell me my artistic lifestyle has merit. I know they love me, even if they don't quite appreciate why I need to be different from them.'

Over a period of weeks, and after joining a support group of creative individuals, Carla came to realize that 'I don't have to keep asking my family for validation or approval of who I am. What I really want from our family get-togethers right now is to enjoy whatever moments of connection and warmth are possible while my parents are still alive. I've got to make sure Kevin's nonsense doesn't take that away from me.'

MOVING FROM INTIMIDATION TO EMPATHY

Okay, so now that you know what *not* to do, what *can* you do to try to change a stressful pattern of interaction with a particular relative? The first and most powerful step is to change what you say to yourself about this person's obnoxiousness. For years Carla had viewed Kevin's criticisms and sarcastic remarks as being dangerous comments about her own inadequacies. To change this painful situation, I asked Carla to do some quick research. I urged her to find answers to a few important questions that you, too, should consider when dealing with your own difficult relatives.

What could his problem be?

I suggested that Carla should try and find out what happened in Kevin's early years that could have made him so bitter and attacking? When Carla talked to her sister Julie and one of Kevin's younger sisters about this, she discovered some valuable information. It turned out that when Kevin was very young he was considered unattractive and gawky. At school he was rejected by the popular girls and he was always picked last in sports by the team captains. Only in his thirties, when he began to make substantial money in business, did Kevin begin to blossom into someone who could successfully find a date and be invited to play golf or tennis by his work colleagues. Yet his insecurities and bitterness were probably still churning around inside.

Does he or she have a nice side?

What's your problem relative like when he or she's being nice? Admittedly, it may be hard to imagine him being fun, creative, affectionate, vulnerable, helpful or kind when he picks on you all the time. Yet when Carla talked to her sister Julie and one of Kevin's old friends about this, she found out that Kevin did have a pleasant side to him. Julie told a story about when she was very ill, during the last four months of her difficult pregnancy with her second child. Kevin not only got up in the middle of the night and early in the morning to care for their older child, but he also brought flowers and prepared vitamin smoothies that he brought to Julie in bed each morning. One of Kevin's oldest friends also mentioned that

Kevin was often the only person to make an occasion out of friends' birthdays. According to this friend, 'We all know Kevin can be a complete jerk at times, but he's also loyal and dedicated to the people who are closest to him.'

What about you threatens this individual?

This was the most helpful question Carla asked about Kevin. She had always thought of him as intimidating and threatening, so she couldn't imagine that he might in fact be threatened or intimidated by her. Then she had a heart-to-heart conversation one night on the phone with her sister Julie, during which Carla asked, 'Is there something about me or the way I live my life that might be threatening to Kevin?'

Julie thought for a moment and responded, 'That's an interesting question. I don't think I've ever told you that Kevin always wanted to be a musician. He worked really hard at it, and he played guitar in a cutting-edge band at school and college. But they couldn't make much of a living from their music. So he stopped playing entirely. He hasn't picked up a guitar for over twelve years.'

Carla thought she heard a touch of sadness in Julie's voice as Julie explained, 'I suppose Kevin feels uncomfortable and maybe even a little intimidated when he sees you sticking to your art. It probably makes him wonder if he gave up on his creative side too soon, or maybe he resents you for becoming what he couldn't become. Or maybe he thinks he's protecting you from the disappointment he suffered and that's why he's always trying to give you too much advice.'

After finding out a little about Kevin, Carla felt the beginnings of a shift in the way she viewed him. As Carla told me in a counselling session, 'I still don't like the man, and I can't condone the way he talks to me. There ought to be a finishing school for adults where they teach basic human decency to men like Kevin, who don't seem to understand the concept. But for the first time in years I don't feel intimidated or as easily hurt by him anymore. I almost feel sorry for him, and I'm glad he has a few friends and my sister Julie who understand his inner turmoil and his vulnerabilities.'

The next week Carla saw Kevin at a family event, and she later told me how her perception has changed. 'It feels different watching Kevin in action now after learning more about his past. There was a birthday dinner the other night for my mother and, as usual, Kevin made a stupid remark about what I was wearing. Yet it didn't have much of an impact on me this time. His comment was almost like static on the radio or someone breaking wind. Not pleasant, but not a very big deal. It felt like a breakthrough that I could hear him say something designed to upset me and I could remember that it was more about his insecurities than about mine.'

As Carla and many of my counselling clients have discovered, even the most verbally abusive and intimidating person is usually mush inside. Like a cactus that has sharp needles on the outside to protect the soft, fragile inside, most of our difficult relatives have developed prickly layers and defensiveness to keep their inner psychological wounds a closely guarded secret.

I urge you to do some quick research and find out if the person who has caused you years of discomfort and pain is actually someone much more vulnerable than you've ever imagined. Instead of fearing this person or feeling inferior to him or her, it might be more appropriate to feel sadness or compassion.

FINDING THE RIGHT WORDS

Once Carla was no longer feeling intimidated by Kevin, I asked her if she would be willing to have a face-to-face conversation with him about improving their relationship. At first she was hesitant. She commented, 'Why would I want to spend any time with this person when he's consistently so unpleasant?'

I explained to Carla that the goal of a face-to-face conversation is not to become best friends; nor is the goal to change this person's underlying personality or his way of behaving. Rather, the goal is to see if there is the possibility of a small amount of improvement. In some family conflicts, the goal might be to make this person 10 per cent less obnoxious, or to make it possible that a family get-together will be 20 per cent more enjoyable. Even a small amount of progress will make your family gatherings that much less painful.

Carla was still hesitant. 'I don't think there are any "right words" to say to Kevin,' she said. 'He can turn whatever you say into another joke or another attack. He's impossible to talk to, and I don't relish the idea of making myself available for him to chop me up again.'

I offered Carla a choice, as I do with all my counselling clients who are unsure about whether to have a face-to-face conversation with an unpleasant family member. I told her, 'If you decide not to talk to Kevin about how to improve things, I'll respect your decision. Taking care of yourself by decreasing your contact with Kevin is a perfectly reasonable choice, especially if your intuition tells you there is no hope of any progress with him. On the other hand, I would love to explore what might be the right responses for dealing with someone as verbally poisonous as Kevin.'

Carla thought for a few moments and said, finally, 'I'm willing to give it a try.' So we practised a few responses and non-threatening phrases that might open Kevin up to making a slight improvement in the way he treats Carla at family events. Here are the words that have worked for many individuals. See if any of these feel right for your situation.

Asking for help

If you want to soften someone's hard heart and build better rapport with a relative who has been very harsh or difficult in the past, one of the gentlest and most effective phrases is to say, 'You and I both want our family gatherings to be more enjoyable and less stressful. I need your help and your advice. Tell me what you think will make things a little better the next time we get together for a family event.'

You will notice that these disarming, non-threatening words put aside the past. They bypass the personality clashes. They avoid troublesome words like 'always' and 'never'. They are a direct invitation for the other person to start thinking positively and constructively about how to improve things.

This technique was developed many years ago by experts and consultants who advise companies on how to deal with irate customers. Instead of arguing with an angry customer or telling him to 'Lower your voice' or 'Don't be so angry' – two phrases that often make the angry person start shouting even louder – the most effective response is to calmly ask the upset individual to explain slowly and carefully what advice he or she would give you to improve the situation. By letting the other person speak first, and by listening to each idea or suggestion with seriousness and respect, you will turn an angry adversary into a more relaxed and cooperative individual. The best customer service representatives and customer relations professionals are the ones who can listen so caringly and attentively that the irate customer instinctively knows it's time to calm down.

This same technique works extremely well with angry, stubborn or obnoxious family members. If you make the mistake of saying 'Lower your voice' or 'Calm down', your relative will probably shout even louder. On the other hand, if you imagine yourself to be a well-trained customer relations specialist who knows how to calm an irate and verbally provocative customer, you can see yourself not as a helpless victim but rather as a competent and caring professional. With the calmest and most respectful voice you can muster, you might then say, 'You and I both want our family gatherings to be more enjoyable and less stressful. I need your help and your advice. Tell me what you think will make things a little better the next time we get together for a family event.'

If the difficult family member doesn't immediately come around, just keep imagining yourself to be a powerful and well-trained customer relations expert. Calmly and warmly remind the other person, 'I'm listening. I do want to understand what you're saying. What do you think will make things better?' By managing and directing the conversation in this way, you keep it positive and goal-orientated. It might look like you are being soft or compliant, but in fact you are taking charge. Sooner or later, even the most difficult family member is likely to offer some ideas on how to make the next family event less stressful.

Here's what happened when Carla tried out this first phrase with Kevin. Carla called him on the phone one evening and asked if he had a minute to offer her some advice. Kevin jumped at the chance. Then she repeated the phrase we had practised. 'You and I both want our family gatherings to be more enjoyable and less stressful. I need your help and your advice. Tell me what you think will make things better the next time we get together for a family event.'

At that point, Kevin made an obnoxious and sarcastic remark, telling Carla, 'It'll be a lot better if you lose ten pounds and you wear a dark thong under a see-through dress.'

But Carla didn't take the bait. Staying calm and strong, she said simply, 'Well, that's one idea to consider. And I know we both want things to improve at our family gatherings. I do need your help and your advice. What do you think might improve things?'

Kevin was quiet for a moment. Then he listed six different things that he thought would make the next family event less stressful for everyone. As Carla told me a few days later, 'Some of Kevin's ideas were ridiculous, but I just listened respectfully and let him know I was taking him seriously. Surprisingly, a few of his ideas were pretty good. I told him I liked one of his ideas a lot. That seemed to soften him a bit. I never realized it before, but it's quite possible that Kevin desperately wants me to like him and approve of him. But he's got an awfully bizarre way of trying to win me over. He's like one of those nine-year-old boys who punches his friend in the arm or the stomach as a way of bonding or getting closer. As Kevin and I talked for several minutes about his ideas and my ideas on how to improve things in our family, I got the sense that he had wanted this kind of closeness for many years but he'd done all the wrong things to try to get me to like him. What a sad situation that people in our families want to connect but they do the very things that will make connection impossible.'

A few weeks later there was another family event, and Carla said she was anxious to see if there would be any improvement as a result of her phone conversation with Kevin. 'For the first few hours everything went fine. Kevin was more civil and less obnoxious than I've ever seen him. But true to form, he did make a couple of hurtful comments near the end of the evening. I'd say overall it was a 50 per cent improvement.'

As Carla's story illustrates, the goal is not to change your relative completely or to expect a 100 per cent improvement. But if you initiate a conversation where both you and the other person can brainstorm on how to make things better at your family events, you will probably see at least a little benefit.

The caring sandwich

In an ideal world, you would never have to ask for anything from your most difficult family member. But sometimes you do need this person to help you out and there's no way of escaping it.

For example, one afternoon Carla came into my office and told me she unfortunately needed something very important from Kevin and she was unsure of how to talk to him about it. She was planning to bring her new boyfriend, Roger, to a forthcoming family do that she was hoping would be a positive first meeting for Roger and her family. She had warned Roger about Kevin, but still she was worried that Kevin might somehow go out of his way to ruin this important occasion.

As Carla described it, 'I've begun to have anxious thoughts in the middle of the night about bringing Roger to meet my crazy family for the first time. It's risky because I think Roger might be more than just another boyfriend. It feels like he might be my future husband, unless my family or something else starts to drive us apart. So I don't want Kevin saying things about me to Roger that will humiliate me. And I would prefer it if Roger were to meet my entire family at an event that goes well, instead of the usual fiasco where ugly scenes and hurtful words leave everyone feeling bad.'

While I reminded Carla that there is no guarantee of being able to change or control a difficult relative, especially someone as habitually rude and insensitive as Kevin, we did explore a second way of approaching Kevin that has been effective for many of my clients. Though it doesn't always succeed, it can help get your needs considered more seriously and may encourage your difficult relative to be on his or her best behaviour at least for a short time after your talk.

I call this powerful but non-threatening communication technique the Caring Sandwich because it consists of two caring comments surrounding and buffering an assertive statement or request in the middle. Once you understand the concept, you can use this approach whenever you're being assertive and asking for something specific from a difficult relative.

The Caring Sandwich that Carla and I developed for getting Kevin to control himself and be less obnoxious at the family dinner had three parts:

'I respect you'

As the name suggests, the Caring Sandwich has a bottom, a middle, and a final component to top it all off. The bottom, or foundation, of the Caring Sandwich is the positive statement you make in order to soften the tough heart of this difficult relative. Start out by mentioning some aspect of this person's life that you admire or enjoy. Even if you don't like most of what you know about this troubled individual, it's crucial that you find something positive and true to say as the first part of your request.

In Carla's case, the Caring Sandwich began with her calling up Kevin a few hours before the family event to which she would be bringing Roger. After asking Kevin how his family was doing, Carla said, 'Kevin, I respect you for being a great husband to my sister and an amazing Dad with your two kids. I know you've got a good heart.'

Note that Carla said these words with sincerity and genuineness. It's very important that the foundation of your Caring Sandwich be made with positive statements that you feel are true, or else you will sound insincere and manipulative. If you have trouble coming up with anything positive or caring about your difficult relative, you may need to ask others to help you find the spark of goodness and decency that exists deep inside even the most unpleasant human beings   but that may get thoroughly hidden by layers of difficult traits and habits.

'I really hope you'll say only positive things about me'
The next words out of your mouth must be a gentle and clear request explaining what you need this person to do. Without accusing, attacking, blaming or lecturing, you simply need to find a few brief words that describe exactly what you hope he or she will do this time to prevent a painful incident. In Carla's case, the middle portion of her Caring Sandwich was the direct but tactful request, 'I need your help with something very important. I'm bringing a new person to the family dinner and I really hope you'll say only positive things about me and the family so that my friend Roger will get a good impression of all of us.'

'I know you can do this'
The final words out of your mouth should be a positive, supportive comment that you are confident this person can and will come through today. It's like a pep talk from an encouraging coach. In Carla's phone conversation with Kevin, she said, 'I know you can do this. I've seen your caring and your compassion. I hope you can help me out and make today a happy event without any friction.'

By carefully constructing your Caring Sandwich, what you say can focus your family member on doing the right thing at a family event.

Here's what happened at Carla's family gathering. While driving with Roger to the event, she explained in greater detail some of the past difficulties she'd had with Kevin and what her quick research had taught her about some of the sources of Kevin's insecurities and hostile comments. Roger listened carefully and then replied, 'Don't worry. I'm not going to freak because you've got some difficult people in your family. I've got some real characters in my family, too. I promise not to hold you responsible for any disasters that happen at a family event. That's what families are all about. And as for Kevin, if he says anything obnoxious about you, I'll just ask one of my cousins to beat him up.' When Carla looked at him, Roger smiled and said, 'Only kidding'.

At the event, Kevin was more cautious and restrained than usual. Carla told me later that Kevin almost seemed to be trying to win her approval. 'He did make a few obnoxious jokes about politicians and the private lives of film stars, but for the first time in years he avoided saying anything hostile towards me.'

Every situation and every family is slightly different. You may find when using the Caring Sandwich that it works beautifully some of the time to help a difficult family member take your needs more seriously. But at other times your relative's troubled personality or self-centredness might reveal itself once again no matter what you do or say. What's most important about the Caring Sandwich, however, is that it doesn't make things worse. It's a non-threatening way to be assertive without provoking a new round of attacks and counter-attacks. It gets the other person's attention and invites him or her to be a cooperative ally, at least for a short amount of time. If you practise using it, you will find it is one of the most effective ways of bringing out the best in people who otherwise seem intent on showing off their most awful traits.

RESPONDING TO WORST-CASE SCENARIOS

In some cases there is nothing you can say to sway certain family members. It might be a moody teenager who stubbornly refuses to listen to anything you say, or a self-absorbed parent or in-law who chronically lacks the ability to take your needs seriously or empathize with your point of view. Or it might be a dogmatic or self-righteous relative who habitually refuses to see that there are two sides to every family conflict, or a psychologically wounded member of your family who often cannot hear even your gentlest comments without feeling highly insulted or becoming instantly defensive.

What can you do when this difficult relative has shut you out and yet you need some cooperation from him or her? What might resolve this impasse without making matters worse? Here are two options to consider when things get especially nasty.

Let go

What if you were to give up any expectations that this person might be different? What if you were to let go of the idea that he or she can be changed or improved?

This may sound pessimistic, but often if you completely stop trying to change, outsmart or manipulate your difficult family member, some interesting things happen. You free yourself from having to be this person's judge, jailer or rehabilitation coach. You also will feel relief at not having to work so hard to get along with this person. Your brain can stop trying so hard to 'work it out' if you truly give up all efforts to change this individual.

What does it mean to let go? If you are a spiritual or religious person, you may find that a renewed sense of clarity and strength emerges if you stop planning for a while and instead pray, meditate or visualize in silence. Extensive research over the past twenty years has demonstrated that if you let yourself breathe gently in silence to attain a peaceful acceptance of a painful situation that is beyond your control, you can sometimes reach a higher awareness about what's really going on. A sense of divine healing energy or deep intuitive clarity may allow you to break out of your agitation and help you attain some new insights about the situation in your family. I have found repeatedly in my own life and with many of my clients that sitting in silence and focusing on the breath, or on a vision of warm healing light from a higher source, can bring new creativity to the problem of dealing with life's toughest challenges.

But if you are not comfortable with terms like divine healing energy, higher source or peaceful acceptance, there is also a scientific/psychological explanation for this same phenomenon of letting go in order to see things more clearly.

Twenty-five years ago, a brilliant Gestalt psychologist and prominent researcher from UCLA in the United States, Arnold Beisser developed and studied the effectiveness of something he called *the paradoxical theory of change.*

Beisser asked a number of men and women who were dealing with a difficult challenge to imagine themselves relaxed, calm and centred while *not* trying to change the problem whatsoever. These individuals practised the art of letting go, fully accepting that they were in the middle of a painful and upsetting situation that they couldn't control. Based on his research, Beisser concluded that the best way to change a painful situation is first to become centred, calm and unhurried about where you are, at least for a few moments. Giving your mind and body a brief sabbatical will open up new avenues of insight and creative perspective. Beisser's theory has been used successfully by hundreds of therapists and thousands of clients over the years.

You could think of Beisser's theory in terms of how to get your car out of a one- or two-foot pile of snow. If you aggressively put your car in gear, put your foot down hard on the accelerator, and go for it, you only get deeper into a snowy rut. Your wheels spin and you go nowhere. But if you calmly accept that you are in a rut and you gently rock your car back and forth, back and forth, between reverse and forwards, your vehicle usually finds enough traction to move out of the snowy trap. It's not about racing forwards, but rather about calmly assessing the spot you are in. In a similar way, using prayer, meditation, guided visualization or Beisser's paradoxical theory of change during a painful family conflict can provide you with the necessary traction, patience and gentleness to transform a situation where forceful action often makes things worse.

So whether you think of letting go as a spiritual practice or a psychological/scientific technique, it can be highly effective in helping us break out of old ruts to see things from a new and more innovative perspective.

'The more we tried, the bigger the wall he built to keep us out'

What if you had a troubled relative who consistently lied to you, ignored your good advice and tried to manipulate you? What if you had been trying for years to make an impact on this person and each time you felt completely thwarted?

I once suggested the let-go approach to a client of mine named Rory, a 29-year-old social worker who had spent many years feeling frustrated from trying to manage his troubled younger brother, Philip, 27, an extremely charismatic but highly elusive and manipulative individual who had been in and out of jail several times for using and selling drugs. Rory and his parents had tried nearly everything to help Philip: tough love, expensive treatment centres, various pharmacological remedies, daily phone calls and respected drugs counsellors. Rory told me that nearly every day he felt upset and burdened by the mess Philip had made of his life. But, he said, 'The more we tried, the bigger the wall built to keep us out.'

Rory was surprised when I asked him, 'What would happen if you stopped for a few days or a few weeks and simply let go of the need to change your brother? What if you *had* to accept him exactly as he is? I realize letting go is not an easy thing to do, but if you were to use prayer, meditation or guided visualization, you might be able to see your brother not as a stubborn problem to be fixed, but somehow in a new and different light.'

'Are you saying I should become passive and just let my brother's situation get worse?'

'No,' I said, 'I'm not saying be passive or abandon your brother. Something happens inside the mind when learn to let go, stop trying to work things out and just breathe in and out calmly while accepting things exactly as they are with no agitation or impatience. If you are willing to practise using prayer, meditation or visualization to get beyond your frustration and irritation, you might open yourself up to new and highly effective ways of dealing with your brother.'

Although he was a bit sceptical, Rory said he was willing to try this approach. Over a period of several weeks he began sitting in silence for ten minutes each day with the intention of opening up his heart and his mind to a different way of looking at the situation with his younger brother. Rory admitted this wasn't easy. 'Most of the time when I sit in silence, my brain starts racing with thoughts and angry feelings about my brother and how much I want to tell him what to do.'

I assured Rory that this 'brain noise' is a normal response and that everyone who prays, meditates or uses guided visualization finds his or her mind drifting, especially in the early stages of learning how to let go. When you notice your mind racing, it doesn't mean you're doing anything wrong. It just means you should go back to noticing your breath moving softly in and out of your body as you go deeper into silence.

Rory decided to stick with the ten-minutes-a-day routine, and after a few weeks he did experience a higher percentage of peaceful moments. Then, during one of these silent sessions, something unusual happened.

Rory told me during his next appointment, 'I was sitting in my room, meditating with less brain noise than usual, and

I started to have a memory of a warm sunny day where my brother Philip and I were just relaxing on the beach. At that moment, I sensed a deep connection with Philip and I noticed a few tears in my eyes.'

He continued, 'It sounds strange, but the feeling I had was that on some level Philip and I aren't really separate beings who are at odds with each other. I don't know exactly how to say this, but it was as though Philip and I share a deep connection, almost like we're part of the same whole. It's hard to explain, but for an instant I felt completely at peace with who he is, and I had this thought that Philip's path in life and my path in life are somehow meant to be. I began to feel so much less judgmental of him and all he's been going through. After years of wanting to grab him and shake him, I had a moment of feeling a lot of love and acceptance for my little brother. It was the first time I saw him as a pure soul who's trapped inside a very addicted body. And then I imagined Philip looking me in the eye and saying, "Don't judge me, Rory. In this lifetime I ended up with the messed-up bio-chemistry. In the next lifetime, it could be you with the addictive urges, and then you might need my support and patience."'

That meditation experience was the beginning of a breakthrough in Rory's relationship with Philip. As he describes it, 'There are still challenging moments, but something changed in the way I've talked to him ever since that silent meditation when I felt our connection in a new way. Philip tells me I no longer sound as impatient, judgmental or self-righteous as I apparently had become towards him for many years. Now when we talk on the phone or see each other in person, he says he feels like I'm an ally instead of a "patronizing twit". So he's begun to let down the wall that

he'd put up for a long time. That's not to say things are perfect with Philip. I still wouldn't feel happy lending him
money or letting him babysit for my infant daughter. Philip's
still battling his inner turmoil, his drug cravings, and I can
sense at times he's still tempted to go back to his lifelong
habit of manipulating people.'

A few weeks later, Rory told me during his final session,
'The good news is that Philip's been drug free for 26 days so
far, but I don't know what will happen. Whether he stays
clean or not is beyond my control. But lately he's been really
honest with me and we've become very close, like brothers
again. The shift in the way I see him has helped us stop getting on each other's nerves so much.'

Can letting go through a technique such as prayer, meditation or guided visualization cause a breakthrough in your
relationship with an extremely difficult relative? I have seen
that for some clients it has made a huge difference, while for
others nothing much seems to happen.

In Rory's case, learning to let go not only helped him
become less judgmental and more successful with his brother,
but it also helped Rory become a less rigid and more effective
social worker. As he told me in a phone call a year after he
completed his counselling sessions, 'I realize now that I used to
be a bit too self-righteous and impatient with my social work
families. Just like I was somewhat patronizing and judgmental
with Philip, I was that way in my professional life as well. Letting go with Philip taught me how to connect on a more profound level with the families I'm trying to help in my work.'

I have found that quite often the hard-earned lessons we
gain from fully accepting our difficult family members help
us in other areas of our lives as well. The struggle to overcome
our own impatience and rigidity in our family interactions

often leads to less impatience and rigidity in our work and even our romantic relationships. You might want to think of your frustrations with your relatives as being like the abrasive sand in an oyster's shell that helps create a valuable and stunning pearl. We don't know ahead of time what kind of growth or pearl will emerge from these encounters, but in hindsight, they often are important breakthroughs.

Each person reading this book has to decide for herself whether she really wants to try to fully accept her family members as vulnerable human beings. Each reader has to look inside and make his own assessment of whether he wants to explore spiritual, religious or unconventional techniques as a possible option when things get nasty with a relative. I can't tell you what to do, but I hope you will consult your own spiritual, religious or psychological advisors, along with books, teachers and your own inner feelings, to find out what might work for you in dealing with difficult family members.

Call for back-up

Besides letting go, another option that can help break an impasse with an especially stubborn relative is what I refer to as calling for back-up. In many family conflicts, a relative may not listen to you but he or she will listen to someone who has certain power or authority.

It could be a priest or rabbi who can call, write or talk in person to your difficult relative and say, 'I'm concerned about your family and I need you to do the right thing.' Or it could be the best friend of your problem relative, who can look him or her in the eye and say, 'Cut it out.' It might be an older member of the family who has enough status and influence to be able to say, 'Stop it right now.' Or it might be a counsellor, lawyer, doctor, social worker or other professional person who has enough of a track record and enough clout with your difficult relative to be able to say, 'Listen to me. This is what you need to do.'

In the field of family therapy, this calling for assistance is considered a controversial approach. Throughout the past three decades, there has been a trend in the profession against what is called *triangulation*, psychologists' jargon that means if you are Person A and you have a conflict with Family Member B, you mustn't expect Person C to speak up on your behalf or solve the problem with Family Member B for you. Some family therapists think that talking to Person C when you have a problem with Family Member B is weak or manipulative. Some family therapists forbid their clients to ask an outsider for assistance. These therapists believe we must fight our own battles and confront face-to-face the people in our family who have wronged us. They insist that unless you talk to Family Member B directly and resolve the problem on your own, you will not be fully healed or empowered.

While I agree that as a general rule it's preferable to deal with people directly and not to go behind their backs, there are certain family conflicts and crises that require a different approach. For example, Rita's case is a clear illustration of when it's appropriate and extremely effective to call for backup. If you have a relative as difficult as Rita's mother, you might want to consider using a similar approach.

'She's a difficult woman'

Barbara is Rita's mother. A very attractive, stylish and intelligent sixty-two-year-old woman with a fiery temper, Barbara has been divorced three times. When you first meet her, you notice how cultured and charming she is. Barbara has two living children, Rita, 33, and a younger son, Bruce, 31, who moved several years ago to New Zealand. Barbara's first child, Gayle, died in a car accident almost 20 years ago, an event that still weighs heavily on the family.

My client Rita is the programme director of a charity that helps homeless and battered women find shelter, clothes, job training, better incomes and increased self-respect. Rita and her fiancé, Eric, have been together for three years, and they decided seven months ago to get married.

According to Rita, 'Eric and I knew when we started to plan our wedding that my mother was going to be difficult. But we had no idea it would get this bad. My mother says to her friends that she's proud of my work with homeless and battered women, and yet she gets extremely upset and vindictive every time she calls my mobile phone and doesn't get an immediate answer. She'll either stop talking to me for a week or she'll call a couple of hours later and say, "You are the most uncaring daughter. I called you at four o'clock and you didn't even pick up the phone. Where were you?"'

Whenever her mother attacks her for not picking up the phone, Rita feels caught in a no-win situation. She explains, 'If I tell Mum I was in a meeting, she will either slam the phone down or else stay on the line and say tearfully, "I thought you were dead."' Rita admits, 'When she does that, I'm never sure if Mum is feeling the pain from when my sister Gayle died in a car accident or whether she is just being dramatic and controlling. It's very hard to know whether you should feel compassion for her pain or whether you should be protecting yourself against her manipulation.'

A few weeks before Rita's wedding, an incident occurred that resulted in Rita seeking counselling. Rita and Eric had decided that they wanted to invite Rita's father (Barbara's first husband) to the wedding. Rita told me, 'He is my father and I love him a lot. Even though he and Mum have hated each other for years, I felt I wanted him to be included at this important gathering. But I also knew this might infuriate Mum, so Eric and I took her out to a nice restaurant and explained to her very carefully how we want this to be a good event for her, too. And we asked her in the nicest way if there was any possibility she might accept my father being at the wedding – perhaps at a separate table at the reception.'

According to Rita, 'I've never seen Mum as hurt and upset as she was then. She stormed out of the restaurant and has refused to talk to me ever since, except to leave a message on my voicemail to say she will not be coming to the wedding. I don't know what to do. Part of me says to just let her make her own choices and hope that the wedding will be fine without her. Another part of me says I need to apologize because it will feel strange to have a big family gathering and Mum not there. If I think about what I really want, it's very clear – I want to find a way to get my mother to turn up and behave herself at my wedding. But whenever I try to call her to talk about it, she hangs up on me. How do I break through?'

When I explored with Rita if there was anything she could do or say differently to help her mother come to the wedding, Rita explained, 'My mother is very proud. If she says she's not coming to the wedding, there's nothing I can do to change her mind. Besides, she won't talk to me on the phone and she sent back the affectionate note I sent her last week. She's a difficult woman, my Mum.'

I then asked Rita, 'Is there anyone in your Mum's inner circle who might be able to talk to her and help her calm down between now and the wedding?' Rita thought for a moment but couldn't think of anyone.

So I suggested, 'Is there a member of the clergy who has some influence or any relatives who have some clout?' Rita smiled and said, 'There's no one in the family who hasn't had a row with her. Believe me, if there were someone my mother would listen to, I'd gladly ask them to help out.'

So I inquired, 'Does your Mum have a friend with whom she discusses things and who might be helpful?' Rita replied, 'My mother has several women she goes with to museums or concerts. But I know for a fact they don't give her advice. In fact, one of her friends told me recently, "Your Mum is a very smart woman when it comes to fashion and culture. But I never make the mistake of talking about personal relationships or family issues with her. She always gets upset and that ruins the time we're together."'

I was almost ready to give up, but then I said, 'Can you think of anyone at all who isn't afraid of your Mum?' Rita's face lit up a bit and she told me, 'There is one person who has always been able to answer her back and get away with it. My mother has had the same cleaning woman for almost 20 years. But she's a lot more than a cleaner. Maria's like a surrogate mother for my Mum, and she's been a consistent source of stability in my mother's life. Maria's tough and she doesn't back down when Mum pisses her off. I've seen Maria tell my mother to chill out. I've seen her tease her about eating too many biscuits, and once she even told her she was being a bitch. Maria can say things to my mother that I could never say or get away with.'

Rita arranged a meeting with Maria and asked her, 'Would you be willing to talk to my mother and ask her behave properly at my wedding, even if her ex-husband is in the room?' Maria smiled and said, 'You bet I will. I think it's disgraceful that Barbara has been acting like this. Of course

I'll talk to her. I'm even going to bring my wedding album and my daughter's wedding album. I'm going to show your mother how important these family photos are and tell her how often my grandchildren look at them. Believe me, I don't think Barbara is going to want to be left out of the pictures. This is about much more than an ex-husband, and Barbara needs to wake up and realize what she's going to miss.'

In every family situation there is almost always someone who has the clout to stand up and be effective with even the most intimidating or stubborn relative. If you can't think of who this might be for your difficult family member, ask around. 'Who might be the one person that has some influence or sway with...?'

Several weeks later, Rita and Eric got married. The photographer took lots of candid shots of the ceremony, the dancing and the celebration. But there were also several formal shots of the important members of Rita's family, and Barbara was right there in the middle, looking great after spending time and money getting her hair, her dress, and her hat just right.

As Rita said afterwards, 'It was a fantastic wedding, and my mother knew she needed to behave herself. Very few people at the event had any idea how much drama had taken place leading up to that memorable day. I love my Mum and I hate my Mum. But I'm glad she came to my wedding.'

CHAPTER THREE

FIVE WAYS TO IMPROVE FAMILY GET-TOGETHERS

Each year brings special occasions when relatives gather. At these events, will your family get on, or get on each other's nerves? Will you come away with great memories or frustration headaches?

If the only thing you knew about family gatherings was what you saw in advertisements, you might imagine that all over the country, men and women are sitting down to lovely, stress-free meals with well-behaved relatives. You might get the impression that family celebrations are satisfying and a joy for everyone there.

But if you were to tell the truth about what really happens when *your* extended family gets together for Christmas, birthdays, weddings and so forth, you might recall moments when certain relatives get on your nerves. If you think back to your last few family gatherings, is there some aspect that has needed sorting out for years? Is there some part of a family get-together that leaves a bad taste in your mouth each time, and yet it keeps getting repeated over and over again?

This chapter will focus on how to change the specific elements that need improvement at your family gatherings, and what can be done to make these events more enjoyable and less stressful. Based on the ideas and collective wisdom of thousands of families who have come into my clinic or attended my workshops, I would like to offer a few practical tips for you to consider.

But first, have you ever heard the story about the extra-tender pot roast? Whether you are a vegetarian or a meat lover, this story is about more than just food.

A young woman named Gina, who was going to be hosting a large family gathering, wanted to learn how to make a tender pot roast (her only previous attempt had turned out dry and tough). So she asked her mother for advice on how to make the perfect pot roast, and her mother said, 'You have to cut off the tip – exactly like my own mother always did – and make sure the roast isn't too large. That's the secret for keeping in the juices and making it tender.' Then Gina's Mum showed Gina precisely how to cut off the tip of the roast before putting it in a special pan and cooking it.

Gina did exactly what her mother suggested, but her pot roast came out dry and tough again. So Gina decided to ask her grandmother, who said, 'You just need to cut a little more off the tip. That's what your great-grandmother always did and her roasts were always moist and tender.'

This time Gina carefully did just what her grandmother told her to do, but once again the pot roast came out tough and dry. So she decided to spend some time with her beloved great-grandmother. Gina said to her, 'I want to make an extra tender pot roast – do I need to cut off more of the tip?'

Her great-grandmother laughed and said, 'You think that would help?'

Gina replied, 'Well, Mom and Grandma both said that's how you always did it, and your roasts were amazingly tender.'

The great-grandmother laughed again. 'Gina, darling, do you know why I cut off the tip? I had a very small roasting pan ... no other reason. If you want a tender pot roast, cook it slowly at 275 degrees for six hours and it'll be perfectly tender.'

As in this pot roast story, quite often our families don't remember exactly why an indispensable family routine or habit first started. Like the mother and grandmother in the story, we keep following the barely understood routine and we assume it's the only way to do things. It takes someone like Gina to go and find out precisely why her family has been cutting off the tip of the meat for more than sixty years.

This chapter will attempt to discover if you and your family have been following a similarly misguided notion of what your relatives think will make things 'tender' at family events. Rather than continuing to rely on some habit or family myth that hasn't worked effectively for years, there will be five specific alternatives offered for making sure you come away from family gatherings far more satisfied and far less frustrated.

METHOD ONE: SHORTEN THE LENGTH OF GET-TOGETHERS

Quite often after hearing from friends, colleagues and clients that they had a disappointing time at a family event or long weekend with their relatives, I ask two questions. 'How long were things relatively peaceful before they began to turn sour?' and 'What is your family tradition for the length of a "proper" stay?'

If you take a moment to think of the answers that apply to your own family gatherings, you might be surprised to find you've hit upon one of the most common causes of family conflict: your family visits might last longer than you and your relatives can handle. I learned about this phenomenon first-hand several years ago when I was supervising my son when his friends came to play. As many parents discover from experience, if you arrange a pre-schooler's get together for an hour or two, the children get on well enough. But if you plan a longer visit – say, three or four hours for children that young – then fights and ill-temper are bound to occur.

It's the same for families. During a summer holiday or winter break visit, you and your relatives might get along pretty well for the first three or four days. But if your family has a rock-solid tradition of spending ten days or two weeks together and it usually ends up in fights, well, let's face facts: the duration is too long. Or if experience tells you that a three-hour holiday gathering or festive meal goes somewhat more smoothly than a seven-hour marathon with four hours of pre-meal cocktails and small talk, you don't need an advanced degree in psychology to work out that maybe the three-hour gathering might be a better idea.

Lobbying for change

Here's the catch: it may be easier to pass a new law than to change one of these 'we've always done it this way' family routines. If you were to call your parents, your in-laws or your other relatives and say, 'I've just read a family psychology book where the therapist suggests we may be we'd be better off having a peaceful three-hour Christmas dinner rather than sticking to our seven-hour version, where people drink far too much and become difficult' – in most families that would land you in deep trouble very quickly. How dare you change the way it's been done as far back as anyone can remember? How dare you question a family tradition?

Clearly, these kinds of earth-shattering changes do not usually get accomplished with just one phone call. You may need to lobby several of your family members for months to achieve a consensus that maybe it's time to focus on what works and stop repeating what doesn't. In the families that have successfully changed family gatherings from 'far too long' to 'just right', it usually involved the following specific steps.

1. After a family event that turned ugly because it went on too long, call the sanest members of the family and ask them if they also thought the event was a bit lengthy. Did they notice the three relatives who in the fourth hour got so drunk or overstuffed that their personalities changed or they fell asleep? Did they find that certain irritable relatives were able to stay civil for a limited amount of time, but because the event was so long the civility began to melt away until the nasty arguments and power struggles began to re-emerge? Did anyone observe how the young children in the family did pretty well for the first half of the gathering but were unable to last past a certain point? Did anyone else think that if the event had ended after X number of hours it would have left good memories instead of the painful ones that everyone had? Helping your relatives begin to consider the time element is a crucial first step.

2. Next, you may want to brainstorm with your sanest relatives to decide which of you will be the key spokespeople advocating a change for next time. Which of you has the courage or willingness to speak up? Which of you has the respect and influence in your extended family to get the most powerful family members to see your point of view? How many of your sanest relatives are willing to volunteer to talk gently and lovingly to the one member of the family whom

you can anticipate will be devastated by even the possibility of changing the family routine?

3. Finally, when you suggest this new idea to the one or two family members who might feel threatened by the notion of changing anything, be sure to tell them that this is not necessarily a permanent change but rather an experiment. Explain it this way: 'We'll see how it goes. If it doesn't improve anything, we can go back to how it was. If it does improve things, we can discuss whether to run the experiment again, or just go back to the traditional version.' This promise of a one-off experiment must be sincere, though. If, after giving it a chance, your reluctant relative doesn't think there's been enough improvement, then you may have to compromise and let the old ways prevail.

'Far too many drinks and nibbles'

I once counselled a woman named Evelyn who told me, 'In my family it's traditional for every Christmas to be a seven-hour event. The cousins, aunts, uncles, grandparents, in-laws and other relatives turn up at my mother-in-law's house around 2 pm and we spend the next four hours having far too many drinks and nibbles, until by the time dinner is served around 6 pm, the scene has become very unmanageable. The children are out of control, the grown-ups are exhausted and the three problem drinkers in the family are getting boring or bad-tempered.'

Evelyn described how 'for years we begged my mother-in-law to make it shorter or serve the meal earlier. But each time she would start crying and say, "This is how it was in my family when I was a little girl. We came at two o'clock and we ate at six o'clock. How can you ask me to give up one of my favourite memories from my childhood?"'

Evelyn told me she was very frustrated at her mother-in-law's inflexibility. She also said, 'My mother-in-law is totally rewriting history. We all know there was serious alcoholism and even some abuse in her family. But my mother-in-law can sit there and say with a completely straight face, "Don't make me change how wonderful it was when I was a little girl."'

In many families, there is a myth about how the holidays were perfect long ago. That need not be your concern. Many of our relatives live in a state of denial, and you can't force them to give up their rewritten memories. Our difficult and troubled relatives are going to remember the past however it suits them, truthful or not.

But what helped Evelyn's mother-in-law to relax a little was for Evelyn, Evelyn's husband, his sister and one other sibling to offer a one-off experiment. In a calm and non-threatening tone of voice at a family meal two months before Christmas, Evelyn and these other members of her husband's family suggested to Evelyn's mother-in-law, 'We're not asking for a permanent change in the Christmas tradition. Let's just try an experiment this once. Let's have a meal where we all help you out. People can arrive at 4 pm and we'll serve dinner by 5.30. Then we'll look and see if the children, the feuders, the problem drinkers and the others do better this time. If it doesn't work, we'll go back to the way it's always been. All we're going to do is try and see if we can make this Christmas even better than the good memories we all have.'

Needless to say, the shorter gathering wasn't perfect. There were still a few stressful moments and one particular relative who was being difficult. But overall, Evelyn found, 'It was 75 per cent better than any previous holiday event. There was much less chaos and far fewer uncomfortable moments.

All of us went home feeling close and connected instead of exhausted and resentful. My mother-in-law even got four phone calls from family members who said it was the best Christmas dinner they can remember.'

During the weeks following this experiment, Evelyn found that her mother-in-law was still a little unsure of whether she wanted to commit to doing the shorter version again the next year. 'She told us, "I love the feeling of savouring a whole day spent together with the people I care about most." I was tempted to scream at her and say, "Can't you see how great it was this year and how awful it's been for so long?" But I knew we had sincerely meant it when we promised her that this was a one-time experiment with no obligation to make it permanent.'

Evelyn thought she would have to compromise, but then something wonderful happened. 'My mother-in-law usually won't take advice if it comes from me, but she's a lot more compliant if the advice comes from my husband. So I kept my mouth shut and didn't get into a power struggle with her. But then my husband said to her, "Mum, I've had three more phone calls from relatives who say this was the most enjoyable holiday gathering we've ever had. Are you sure you want to go back to the seven-hour version, which caused so many problems?" Hearing that from her beloved eldest son, my mother-in-law smiled and said, "No, we don't really need to do the seven-hour version. I'll miss it, of course. But I think I'd rather see my loved ones getting along. It was so satisfying to look out across the room this year and see everyone having a good time at dinner. I'm not blind – I know it was much calmer and easier than it's been for a long, long time."'

METHOD TWO: LOOK FOR A DEEPER SENSE OF CONNECTION

The feelings of frustration and alienation you may have experienced at family gatherings often happen because, in most families, everyone is expected to do the same thing as everyone else, as though one size fits all. For example, if your family loves to sit around a big table to argue about political topics and you don't like arguing about political topics, your chance of family closeness may have been hampered year after year by these heated arguments. Or, if your relatives tend to spend every family gathering glued to the television set watching sport, and you don't enjoy watching sport, then you may feel unable to connect in a deeper way with your sports-obsessed family.

In the same way, sitting around a formal dining room table with the conversation being dominated by a few self-absorbed or highly opinionated individuals is less than fun. Have you ever noticed that certain of your relatives don't seem to care that they're repeating themselves and boring everyone to tears? They simply want a captive audience.

Setting the stage for togetherness

What can you do to change these unpleasant routines? What might make a family gathering more comfortable for those of you who have felt left out in the past? What can you do to make meaningful conversations more likely? Here are a few ideas for you to consider trying at your next family gathering:

Set smaller tables. Persuade the host or hostess ahead of time to put family members at several smaller tables, with less outgoing family members seated next to someone they like, so they can have more intimate conversations. Unlike a large table where one or two relatives tend to dominate, this gives everyone a chance to feel involved and included in mealtime conversations.

Arrange varied activities. In addition to the inevitable political conversations or the television, make sure there are snacks and seats arranged for conversations in other parts of the house. Rather than expecting each person to do what the most dominant relatives think is important, allow for deeper conversations to develop before, during and after the meal.

Ask ice-breaker questions. Whether you are at one large table or a series of smaller tables, start a family tradition where each person has the chance to answer a question that is designed to make each guest feel welcome and to put everyone on an equal footing. For instance, ask each relative to give an answer of one minute or less to a question such as:

- Is there anything that's happened in the past year that you've struggled with and learned from?
- Can you share some recent good news?
- What is your favourite family memory?
- Has a relative who is no longer alive taught you something useful or inspiring?
- What is your greatest hope for the coming year?

This type of question can shift the conversation from boring small talk to deep and profound discussions. Just make sure the question is one that each person at the gathering, child or adult, can answer easily, and that will help each individual feel included as an equal. Plan it so that an articulate family member goes first and acts as a role model for how to answer the question briefly and from the heart.

You may also need to appoint a good-natured timekeeper. The one-minute rule need not be applied rigidly, but there still should be some way to keep long-winded relatives from commandeering the activity. Please note, however, that anyone who doesn't want to speak up can say 'Pass' without criticism or mocking. This is important. Someone needs to state at the beginning of the conversation that it's fine to listen to others and feel a sense of family closeness even if you decide to remain silent.

'People get torn apart at our family meals'
Howard is a 29-year-old computer software designer who always felt left out at his family's celebrations. He told me during one of his first counselling sessions, 'In my family, there are a number of highly educated individuals who love to do battle over politics, social issues and current affairs. It's not that I dislike a good political discussion, but in my family, these political debates are more like a blood sport. My uncle Victor loves to rip to shreds anyone who disagrees with him. So does my older sister Muriel, who's a successful barrister – even at school she never lost an argument. At meals with my family, you only have two choices – keep quiet and watch someone else's point of view get torn apart by one of the more talented debaters, or speak up and risk becoming the next victim.'

When I asked Howard if there were any relatives in his family who might enjoy a less argumentative and more relaxed format for family conversations, he told me, 'Absolutely. My Mum and some of my cousins hate the way people get ripped to shreds at our family meals.'

To begin to change the brutal atmosphere at these gatherings, Howard talked to his mother and several other relatives about instituting smaller tables, diverse conversations and more personal topics at the next family meal.

As Howard told me later, 'My uncle Victor and my older sister Muriel complained that people were "wimping out" by not engaging in the traditional political debates. But what happened instead is that I got a chance to sit at a calmer table with two of my favourite cousins that I don't see very often. We had a great conversation about what we were each struggling with in our lives. I got to know them so much better as a result. It was the most alive and connected I've ever felt at a family dinner.'

METHOD THREE: STAY STRONG AND SELF-AFFIRMING

In some families, the previous few suggestions simply won't work. For many readers of this book, the controlling members of your family aren't going to budge on the right length of visits. They aren't going to allow smaller tables. They won't condone warm, welcoming questions that respect the opinion of each person as an equal.

For many of my friends and clients, the way to improve family gatherings is *not* by changing the external structure but by changing your internal reaction to established family routines. You may have to live with the fact that you don't have enough support to change the vicious way people talk to each other in your family, or for sorting out the frustrating routines that have hampered intimate conversations at family gatherings for years.

The challenge you face at your next family event might be how to stop your own habit of losing your sense of self, or feeling like a helpless child again with your relatives. I have found that even the most successful and intelligent men and women, when faced with certain difficult relatives, tend to revert to feeling as if they were 15 years old. Has that ever happened to you or someone you know? You turn up at a family event fully intending to be the mature, competent adult you are in most other settings. But within minutes you find yourself slipping back into feeling like a frustrated and powerless child again. Everything your family does from that moment on makes you feel even worse. It becomes a painful downward spiral until you can't stand being with these people one minute longer.

That's why it's important to plan ahead and come prepared with some techniques for staying strong and self-affirming, even when you're surrounded by negativity at a family event. Here are a few methods that have worked wonders for many of my clients. You can decide for yourself which of the following might help you feel healthier and less squashed at the next family event.

Bring an ally

Plan to have someone at the gathering who appreciates you and who knows that family events can sometimes shake us to our core. Rehearse ahead of time with this friend or loved one what you will need if you get into a pickle with your family. What should this person do or say – or not do or say – if your relatives start to criticize you, make fun of you, order you around or become unpleasant in one way or another? Do you want your supportive friend or loved one to speak up on your behalf or to remain silent? Do you want this ally to look you in the eye for a moment and communicate non-verbally that you are a worthwhile human being who is still appreciated even though you have a difficult family? Do you want this friend or loved one to go for a walk with you? Or to join you in one of the other rooms in the house to discuss what just happened? Do you want this ally to give you suggestions or to refrain from giving any advice? The more clear you make yourself ahead of time, the more successful you will be in staying strong and not reverting back to childhood at the actual event.

Enlist a long-distance ally you can phone

Sometimes it's not possible to have someone supportive at a family event, but you can still be one 'lifeline' phone call away from someone who understands what you're going through. What I've found with many of my friends and clients is that when things get nasty at a family event, we all need someone who can remind us warmly and honestly, 'I know you are a worthwhile human being, even if your family doesn't think so.' This may sound strange, but it's quite common for even the most successful and healthy individuals of any age or degree of psychological sophistication to lose their own sense of self-worth at stressful family gatherings. If you bring a mobile phone, or if you know where the nearest pay phone is, you can have one or more private conversations that can help you regain your clarity of mind and your inner strength no matter what goes on with your relatives. You just need someone who can listen calmly and remind you, 'Don't worry. You *will* survive your family.' I've found in hundreds of cases that this 'lifeline' phone call makes a huge difference in helping us bounce back from painful or frustrating moments.

Use prayer and guided imagery

Many men and women find that just at the moment when your most difficult family member is saying something invasive or hurtful, it helps enormously to say a prayer that no-one else in the room can hear, such as 'Please, God, help me to remember to breathe and stay strong even when I'm face to face with this person who is so challenging', or 'Please give me the wisdom to know who I am in Your eyes, even when I'm face to face with someone who can't see who I am.' Or you can go the toilet and close your eyes for a moment and imagine yourself on the beach, or feeling strong and surrounded by people who love you and understand you. Just because you happen to be at a stressful family event where someone is saying things that are hostile or critical doesn't mean you can't travel to your spiritual centre or use your imagination to visit a place where you are safe and strong.

'I still tend to lose confidence when I'm with my family'

Naomi is a competent and hard-working marketing executive. She supervises a staff of 14 employees and makes major financial decisions with confidence and good sense. But as she told me when she first came in for therapy a few weeks before a large family gathering, 'Whenever I am with my highly demanding mother, my extremely critical father and my very competitive brothers and sisters, I feel like a powerless four-year-old again. I tell myself before each family event that this time I'm going to keep my cool and not be thrown by the things they do. But no matter what I say to myself before I walk through the door, I still tend to lose my confidence when I'm with my family.'

To help Naomi stay strong and feel good about herself, I offered her the three ideas listed above. She told me she wouldn't be able to bring an ally along because this particular family event wouldn't permit guests. But she decided to have two different 'lifeline' friends ready and prepared in case she needed to call. One friend was someone whom she'd known since primary school and who had seen for herself just how difficult Naomi's relatives can be. The other friend was a colleague from work with whom Naomi had shared personal stories about both of their families. Naomi told me, 'I'm pretty sure I can count on both of these friends to give me a boost of energy because they seem to understand what it's like to come from a very complicated family situation. It's a little risky, but I'm fairly confident that these two friends won't judge me for whatever painful feelings I tell them about during my struggles with my relatives.'

Naomi also discussed with me what kinds of prayer and guided imagery she didn't like as well as what kinds she did like. She told me she didn't find guided imagery helpful if it involved situations that seemed unrealistic. For example, Naomi had once gone to a workshop where the leader told everyone to close their eyes and imagine themselves hugging and going on holiday with their most difficult family member. As Naomi remarked, 'The last thing I want to do is go on holiday with my most difficult relatives. I'm interested in feeling warmth, connection and a sense of shared history with my family members, but hugging them or going on holiday does not appeal, even in a guided visualization exercise.'

So Naomi and I worked on her visualizing herself feeling healthy, strong and positive even when she was sitting at a table with her mother, her father and her siblings. Naomi practised breathing calmly in and out while reminding herself, 'These people cannot control me any longer. I can love them from a safe distance and know that on some level they love me, too.' According to Naomi, 'That visualization exercise also felt like a bit of a stretch, but it was a good stretch. I do want to feel some love for my family, and to know that they also love me. So it helps to picture myself feeling strong, healthy and positive. It's like a boost to my immune system that will help me breathe and feel good about myself when I'm actually with them.'

Finally, we discussed whether or not Naomi wanted to use prayer or spirituality as part of her inner work for staying centred and healthy around her relatives. Like many individuals who have positive and negative feelings about prayer and religion, Naomi told me that only if she wrote a prayer in her own words exactly the way it came from her heart would it work. She commented, 'I don't feel comfortable saying prayers that are formal or stiff. If I'm going to pray, it has to be honest and vulnerable.'

So I asked her to write a passionate and honest prayer that might help her during the hard moments of her approaching family gathering. Naomi came up with the following:

'Mysterious Source of all that is, help me, guide me, keep me strong. I need Your wisdom and Your infinite creative energy. I want to stay open to whatever moments of love are possible with these members of my family. Please help me to ignore whatever is hurtful and to connect with whatever love is hidden deep within our hearts for one another.'

A few days after the family gathering, Naomi came to my clinic and told me what had happened. 'There were several challenging moments that in the past would have wiped me out. But this time I came ready to be resilient and strong no matter what my family tossed into my lap. So, when my mother started off on one of her guilt trips about why don't I take her out to lunch more often, I visualized myself staying strong, healthy and mature, even while sitting across the table from her.'

Naomi continued, 'When my father started commenting on my failed relationships and asking invasive questions about my personal life, I listened for a few minutes until I'd had enough. Then I went and made a phone call to one of my lifeline friends, who said all the right things. In the past, my father's comments could have driven down my self-esteem for hours or days. But this time, with the encouraging words of my friend still very fresh in mind, I went back and had a great conversation with my Dad about work, which is easier for us to discuss. And when my siblings started getting on my nerves, I took a moment to pray silently. Within seconds, I could feel a warmth and a connection to my brothers and sisters. Even though they can be a real pain at times, we do love each other underneath it all.'

Like Naomi, you may need to work with a counsellor ahead of time to prepare the tools that can keep you strong and centred during your next family gathering. Or you might want to experiment on your own by inviting a supportive ally, having a 'lifeline' partner standing by or using prayer and guided imagery. Only you can decide what kind of preparation will help you stay resilient and healthy at your next family encounter.

METHOD FOUR: CHANGE YOUR DEFINITIONS OF SUCCESS AND FAILURE

In certain areas of life, a zero-tolerance policy is appropriate. I remember back in 1986 when millions of people around the world sat down in front of their television sets to watch a courageous teacher named Christa McAuliffe and her fellow astronauts launch into orbit on the *Challenger* space shuttle. It was exhilarating to listen to the countdown and see the

huge rockets fire up for lift-off. Then, unexpectedly, the space
shuttle blew up 73 seconds into the flight. Apparently all it
took was one crucial mistake – an O-ring that didn't seal
properly on an unusually cold day – to trigger that tragic
explosion. A zero-tolerance policy towards error was essential
in that situation.

But what might be an acceptable number of glitches or
problems at a family gathering? What might be a tolerable
number of stresses, unpleasant moments, socially inappropriate remarks or insensitive actions? Is it zero? Or can you
endure one or two irritating moments? How about five insensitive remarks or clumsy actions? What about ten?

Reframing the problem

Quite often I hear from friends and clients that they were
hoping a family event would be perfect, and they were
extremely disappointed when one, two or several things went
wrong. This seems to happen most when expectations are
high, such as when people are planning or attending a wedding, a baptism, a bar or bat mitzvah, a silver wedding
anniversary party or an important birthday celebration. Each
minor irritation or awkward moment tends to feel as if it
might ruin the special event.

Over the years I have recommended a radically different
way of assessing the success of family gatherings. I've urged
men and women who have difficult relatives to set a 'budget'
ahead of time in which five or ten things can go wrong at a
family event and the gathering can still be considered successful and satisfying. In the psychotherapy field, this type of
conscious and intentional change of perspective is called
reframing. To see how it works, consider for a moment how
much calmer and more peaceful you would feel inside if you

had the following 'reframed' definitions of success at a family event.

- Success is when you 'budget' ahead of time to expect five or ten awkward moments with your relatives and you come away surprisingly happy when only three or four things go wrong.
- Success is when you ignore the egotists in the room and you find a way to focus on the gentler souls, the colourful characters and the one or two priceless moments of connection and warmth that occur at even the most imperfect family events.
- Success is when you ignore the trivialities of a family event and you concentrate instead on getting to know at least one person in your family a little deeper.
- Success is when your children or grandchildren obtain some lasting memories of relatives who aren't going to be around for much longer.
- Success is when you set an extremely small but realistic goal each year and appreciate even the slightest amount of progress.

Don't underestimate this last point. Big changes can happen through small steps.

'How high should we set the budget?'

Beth's case illustrates the kind of improvements that are likely to happen if you intentionally change your definitions of success regarding a family gathering. To understand how frustrating family events have been for Beth, you need to know a little bit about her background. Beth grew up in a highly argumentative family; her parents divorced when she was 13. For the next ten years, each family holiday and birth-day celebration became a power struggle. Beth's mother wanted the event to happen in one way, while her Dad and step-mother wanted it to be another. Beth and her two sib-lings desperately wanted there to be some semblance of fam-ily closeness and peace, yet every year there were huge arguments and hurt feelings over the logistics of each family gathering.

Then when Beth got married and had children, she tried to create some stable family traditions, and she hoped she would never have to put her kids through a break-up. But soon after the birth of their fourth child, Beth and her hus-band divorced. Beth's husband admitted he had fallen in love with his administrative assistant at work. Once again, family holidays were a painful source of tension.

As a single mother who knows the emotional cost of family friction, Beth has tried to build close family bonds between her four children. But, she explained, 'Now that my children are growing up and starting to have partners and families of their own, it's very hard to get them all together under the same roof for an important event. At recent cele-brations, there's always someone missing or some dispute in the family that creates tension.'

When I discussed with Beth this unusual step of setting a realistic 'budget' of how many things can go wrong with an event still being considered a success, her first reaction was to laugh. 'Oh, I would have to set a very high budget number, because in our family there's always a lot that goes wrong. My youngest daughter tends to call at the last minute to say she can't make it. I get so disappointed. My two sons are often at odds with each other because of recent business disagree-ments. It breaks my heart to see them fighting. My eldest daughter has an adorable but hyperactive child who often disrupts whatever is going on. And my younger son is married to an extremely self-centred woman who has absolutely no tact. Last year she said to my face, "When you're gone, I'm hoping to be the one who inherits your good china. I just thought you should know that."'

Beth then told me she was preparing herself for the next family gathering, so I asked, 'How high should we set the budget? How many awkward or disappointing moments should we let happen before we get upset?'

Based on past experience, she picked the number twelve. I told her, 'If there are more than a dozen difficult moments, then you can start to worry. But anything less than twelve will just be business as usual – a normal family gathering.'

Using this realistic and somewhat ironic number to help her keep her perspective, Beth went into the family dinner a lot more relaxed. As she told me the following week, 'I was pleasantly surprised that only nine irritating things happened. That was three under budget, and it meant I wasn't my usual tense, vigilant self, trying to make everything perfect. I could finally sit back and enjoy having most of my family gathered together. My youngest daughter called me on the morning of the dinner to tell me she would be coming only for a brief time because she and her new boyfriend were going to a jazz club to see a performer they absolutely "couldn't miss." Normally that would have ruined the whole day for me, but this time I said to myself, "It doesn't matter. I'm still way under budget."

'There were also some difficult moments where my two sons were arguing. In the past, it would have upset me, but this time I knew I was still within the range of a successful event and I let them argue while I relaxed on the living room carpet and played with two of my grandchildren. My eldest daughter looked at me near the end of the evening and said, "Mum, you've been so mellow this year. Are you on Prozac or something?"'

Please note that setting a budget for staying calm even if five or ten minor irritations happen at your family event does *not* mean you will tolerate abusive or dangerous behaviour. You still need to set limits and stand up to relatives who cross the line of decency and respect. But if you enter a family gathering ready to stay positive and not be devastated by a few minor disruptions, you will be surprised at how many more gratifying moments you will be able to enjoy.

METHOD FIVE: UNWIND BEFORE AND AFTER EACH FAMILY EVENT

Sometimes it's not just what happens at the actual family gathering that upsets you or makes you feel drained or ill. Sometimes our lives are so pressured and hectic that we come into a family event close to breaking point. Or we turn up with our immune systems seriously compromised. Or we return to our everyday lives feeling lousy after the gathering because we didn't have enough time to unwind afterwards from the stress.

Do you rush around and burn yourself out just before a family event and then get ill either at the event itself or soon afterwards? What if instead of overloading your diary before a family gathering you were to take a 'mental health day off' to prepare for the event? What if you enjoyed a walk in the countryside, had a massage, took a bath, saw an acupuncturist, talked to a friend or counsellor, worked out at a gym or spent a little time writing in a notebook? What if you set aside the day before and the day after a major family gathering for preparing yourself mentally and then for recovering?

Finding time to unwind

I realize that most of us have hectic lives and can't easily do this. But what about a half-day, or a two-hour slot? Or what about just one hour of self-pampering so you can be relaxed, calm and open at your family gathering? The return is worth it. I know from my own life and from what I've seen in my clients that the simple act of unwinding can make a huge difference in how resilient, creative and loving you will feel when you are with your relatives.

'A very short fuse with my relatives'

Jake is a hard-working film editor who used to feel completely stressed and on edge when he visited his difficult family for Christmas, birthdays and other events. According to Jake, 'In my work on film and television projects with absurd deadlines, you have to beat the clock to get the job done. If it means losing sleep, that's part of the job. Or if it means 20 consecutive hours of staring at a computer screen without a break, that's normal. So it's no wonder that I often show up at a family bash feeling exhausted and crabby. It means I have a very short fuse with my relatives. But they usually deserve it.'

When I first asked Jake if he'd be willing to set aside a day for unwinding before and after major events with his difficult family, he looked at me with disbelief. 'Are you joking? I can't afford to skip work for an entire day.'

So I asked him, 'What about a two-hour block of time?'

Jake thought about it for a moment and replied, 'I'd be willing to do a two-hour bike ride to get rid of my tensions before visiting my family. That's going to have to be good enough.'

In fact, for Jake the two-hour bike rides before and after his next few family events made a significant difference. 'Instead of turning up overtired and crabby as usual,' he said, 'I felt a lot less stressed. I notice that when I go for a bike ride and have a quick shower, I tend to be a lot looser and much less edgy. So when I walked into my cousin's house and heard the familiar sounds of children screaming, my uncles bickering, my Dad trying to run everyone's life and my Mum criticizing my Dad, I actually had a smile on my face. This is my very own barking mad family. Within seconds, I'd said hello to one of my favourite cousins I hadn't seen for a while and I hugged my sister's two children, which is always a treat because her kids are so quick, clever and lovable. I even felt a little sad at the end of the night when my niece and nephew came up to me in their pyjamas and asked if they could sleep at my house one day. I adore these two kids and I don't see them nearly enough.'

As Jake and many others have discovered, if you prepare yourself, even a little bit, to feel healthy and relaxed before a family visit, it can dramatically change how you react to the predictable stressors at your family gatherings. Your relatives will still do what they've always done, but your inner strength and your resilience will help you through. Most importantly, your chances of creating good memories and satisfying moments with your loved ones will be greatly enhanced.

CHAPTER FOUR

WHAT TO DO ABOUT RELIGIOUS DISAGREEMENTS AND PRESSURES TO CONFORM

When I was fourteen years old, my mother died of cancer. A few hours after the funeral, our extended family gathered at my grandfather's house for an evening prayer service. My beloved immigrant grandfather, to whom I was very close, announced it was time for the women to leave the living room so the men could pray in the traditional manner. Unlike my grandfather, I was brought up in a liberal Jewish fashion and so I blurted out, 'No! Mum would have wanted the women to pray as equals.'

My father and my older sister grabbed me, pulled me into my grandfather's bedroom, and said, 'Stop it right now. You're being an obnoxious brat.'

But I couldn't stop. I was fourteen. My Mum had just died. At that moment I didn't want to compromise.

The argument lasted for quite a while, until my grandfather's home advantage sealed the victory for tradition. It was my first introduction to the intensity and discomfort of religious squabbles in families.

Later, as a psychotherapist, I heard about many other clashes between family members who have different spiritual beliefs, or different ways of celebrating their shared religious traditions. Religious disagreements are a major source of friction between even the most loving and considerate relatives, especially today. It's a huge issue because a single family can have one member who is strongly religious, another who is moderately religious, another one or two who are strongly anti-religious, plus loved ones who have married spouses from different religions or denominations. With so much religious diversity, there are bound to be disagreements and hurt feelings every so often. See if any of the following questions strike a chord.

- Have you ever been on the receiving end of a 'well-meaning' relative who couldn't stop trying to push his or her religious beliefs down your throat?

- Have you had unpleasant or painful conversations with loved ones about your differing ideas about God, morality, the Bible, premarital sex, abortion, whether to smack children or other highly emotive issues?

- Have you sometimes felt upset that one of your less-religious family members has been dismissive or insulting towards your own religious beliefs or practices?

- Have you had difficulty arranging an important religious event (such as a christening, bar/bat mitzvah, wedding or funeral) because there were serious disagreements between members of your family?

- Is it hard for the members of your family to agree on where to attend religious services?

- Have you ever had an argument over how to celebrate events – such as Christmas – that have both religious and commercial aspects?

– Have you worried that one of your children or grandchildren is being exposed to a different religious
approach that you disagree with strongly, but that you
have to tolerate because you don't want to offend a relative who favours this approach? Or that your children
or grandchildren are *not* being brought up in a faith or
tradition that you care about deeply?

– Have you ever got into an argument with a family
member about how often to attend services, or religious beliefs and traditions you don't support?

– Have you been surprised when a family member you
thought you knew well became noticeably different
after he or she became deeply involved in an intense
spiritual or religious group? Or has a family member
fallen under the influence of a spouse or partner who
holds religious ideas quite different from those your
family grew up with?

– Have you felt frustrated that some members of your
family consider you strange, wrong or stubborn for
holding beliefs that are different from theirs?

There's something about religion and spirituality that
brings out the most opinionated, rigid or patronizing reactions
in almost everyone. For more than twenty years I've been
working as a consultant for an organization that aims to
improve communication between people with different religious beliefs. We have held dialogues that have included Jews
and Christians discussing their fears and curiosity about each
other; Muslims talking in-depth with non-Muslims; New Age
seekers sharing ideas with more traditional members of organized churches; and even atheists and agnostics exploring

their similarities and differences with believers. Each one of these dialogues was fascinating because when men and women sit down peacefully to explore their religious and spiritual differences, amazing breakthroughs often happen. I found that if specific ground rules and techniques are used for discussing these volatile issues respectfully, the clashing individuals can not only stop fighting – they can also heal long-standing conflicts.

The purpose of this chapter is not to tell you or your family members what to believe or how to express your beliefs. Nor am I going to suggest that one member of your family has 'good beliefs', while another has 'wrong beliefs'. Instead, this chapter will offer proven techniques you can use to help build bridges of communication and to break bread more comfortably with family members whose spiritual or religious ideas are in direct opposition to your own. It's not about debating who's got inside knowledge of holiness or the ultimate Truth; rather, it's about how to become a healthier family of diverse individuals sharing a common bond.

I need to warn you, however, that in pursuing a greater understanding and a more peaceful coexistence with family members whose religious ideas you dislike (or even detest), you will be taking a risk. You might risk seeing the humanity in someone whose ideas about God, morality or spiritual practice offend you deeply. Or you might risk finding out that your own ideas for or against religion are a little elitist or insulting. To delve into such crucial issues as the nature of existence and the purpose of our souls is no simple matter. But I hope this chapter on respecting the religious diversity in our families will not only reduce the friction at your family gatherings but also help you clarify the type of human being you would like to be.

The three-step process described below is based on many years of experience in helping families and individuals work through their religious clashes to reach a higher level of connection and teamwork. I've found that these steps can be extremely effective regardless of the specific religion, degree of religious conviction or lack of religious conviction held by your family members.

What's crucial is that you bring your honesty, your most personal beliefs and your deepest compassion to this process. The best way to build bridges between people of differing beliefs is for each of the individuals to be truthful about his or her religious and spiritual concerns. Whether you consider yourself a strongly religious person, a somewhat spiritual but not very religious person, or a strongly non-religious person, your opinions and experiences are important in each of these three steps. I urge you to be honest with yourself in order to achieve the best results from this process.

EXPLORE YOUR OWN ATTITUDE ABOUT RELIGION

You might be surprised to find that this first step is not about the person who gets on your nerves but rather more about your own possible hidden agenda and your innermost attitude towards your beliefs. Quite often when I mention that step one is to examine your own judgmental tendencies, the reaction from clients and workshop participants is, 'What judgmental tendencies? I'm open-minded. The other person is the one who's judgmental.'

Being honest with yourself

It may be true that the other person is far more judgmental, patronizing or manipulative than you are even on your worst day, but I must still ask you to look within. Ask yourself if you have recently been in a religious dispute or power struggle with a member of your family who might be more religious or less religious than you. If so, bring that person to mind and imagine him or her preaching to you about the religious or moral issue that has the two of you at odds. Then answer these questions honestly.

- Is there something from your own past experience that makes it so difficult for you to stomach this other person's religious ideas?

- Do you ever secretly wish this person would just shut up and never talk to you again about his or her beliefs?

- Do you ever imagine yourself saying or doing something so convincing and inspiring to this other person that he or she looks at you and says, 'You're right and I've been so wrong!'

- Do you ever feel embarrassed or worried that this person will state out loud his or her religious beliefs and people will mistakenly think you agree because you are related?

I do not want to stir up trouble or cause a fight but rather to help you recognize what kind of impatience, frustration and judgmental tendencies we all tend to carry inside just below the surface. If we don't realize our own underlying edginess when discussing religious or spiritual issues, it will slip out sooner or later as sarcasm, condescension, arm-twisting or other forms of disrespect. I've found from experience that it's almost impossible for two family members to work through their religious disagreements if one or both parties are pretending to be 'non-judgmental' when in fact they are seething inside.

'We're both very open-minded'

Susan and Bill's case is a good illustration of how crucial it is to identify your own judgmental feelings if you want to have a breakthrough in resolving the religious friction in your family. See if you can recognize that we all have somewhat hostile or condescending feelings just below the surface about certain religious groups, even if we pretend to be neutral or tolerant.

Susan and Bill have been married for 24 years and they have one child, a 22-year-old son, Evan, who recently got engaged to a 21-year-old woman named Claire. Susan, the mother of the future groom, is a longtime environmental campaigner who grew up in a very liberal family that belonged to an evangelical church. Bill, the father of the future groom, is a committed and innovative developer of affordable low-income housing who grew up a Catholic. But, both Bill and Susan are opposed to many of the conservative teachings of the Vatican.

According to Susan and Bill, they brought up Evan to accept all religions and to judge no one. Yet when Susan and Bill came to see me for counselling, Bill admitted, 'We're very worried about Evan's forthcoming marriage. His fiancée Claire is far more religious than we were expecting. She not only refers to herself as born again, but she says she wants to bring up their children with strict traditional values.'

Susan added, 'I'm hoping this is just a phase Claire is going through. I can't imagine that someone so bright and well-educated could be so old-fashioned when it comes to religion. I'm sure she's going to soften a little as she gets further away from the influence of her parents, who are real Bible bashers.'

(For any readers who are half-asleep; if you didn't wince at Susan's remarks about Claire, please go back and read the previous paragraph again.)

At this point in their counselling, I realized that Susan and Bill, like most of us, had no idea they were being judgmental or condescending toward Claire and her beliefs. Like most religiously liberal people I've counselled over the years, Susan and Bill considered themselves 'tolerant' toward all religions. Yet when I asked them directly if they would be willing to let Evan and Claire bring up their children according to Claire's conservative values, Susan commented, 'You know we're both very open-minded and we would try not to interfere. But frankly we'd be horrified if Claire started taking our grandchildren to some old-fashioned Sunday school.'

Welcome to the complicated world of religious disagreements. As I explained to Susan and Bill, 'I'm so sorry to have to say this, but you don't sound very open-minded. If you're going to play a healthy role in how Evan and Claire bring up their children, you'll need to take a hard look at how judgmental and condescending you appear to be about Claire's beliefs.'

Since I, too, am liberal and have had some painful experiences with individuals who tried to force their beliefs on people I care about, I can identify with Susan and Bill's predicament. We liberals like to think of ourselves as open-minded and flexible, but if someone with a strongly fundamentalist approach starts to affect us or our loved ones, we can quickly find ourselves becoming judgmental. It's an indication that maybe we, too, have some biases and rigidity on the issue of religion. If there's going to be a healthy debate in our families and in society as a whole, we will all have to work through our own feelings of intolerance. We might need to recognize the humanity and the complexity of those with whom we disagree strongly.

So I asked Susan and Bill, 'Are you willing to look at the underlying contempt you seem to have for Claire's background and religious ideas? Are you willing to put in some effort to work toward the open-mindedness and love that will be necessary if there's going to be a positive two-way conversation with your future daughter-in-law about the religious upbringing of your grandchildren?'

I wasn't sure whether Susan and Bill were going to be offended by what I said. While I've found that some people absolutely refuse to consider the possibility that all of us can at times be condescending or judgmental, in this case Susan and Bill were willing to re-examine their own attitudes. As Susan explained, 'We love Evan enormously, and if he wants to marry Claire then we need to learn to understand who Claire is and not to treat her like an unwelcome outsider.'

Bill agreed, and admitted, 'I sometimes pretend I'm calm and neutral about certain religious people and groups, but in fact I carry a lot of baggage from painful past experiences both with family members and teachers who were rigid and oppressive. I suppose that baggage reveals itself sometimes when I meet someone who resembles these characters from my past. A part of me gets furious because I wish everyone could see things the way I do. I don't like to admit it, but at times I can be quite intolerant.'

Now that you've seen Susan and Bill take the first step and re-examine their judgmental tendencies about religion, the decision about what to do next regarding your own situation is yours. Do you want to be like many others who pretend they have no hidden contempt for family members who hold opposing religious and moral viewpoints? Do you want to cling to the idea that you have no secret bitterness towards family members who strongly disagree with your deepest beliefs? If you are liberal when it comes to religion, can you honestly say you don't have some impatience and intolerance towards the more conservative or traditionalist members of your family? Or if you are a conservative or devout individual, do you honestly believe you hold no bitterness inside towards the liberal or secular family members who dismiss or don't understand your beliefs?

The first step in any healthy communication is for both sides to admit that there's some distance to travel in order to see the other person as a worthwhile soul with valid opinions, rather than as an enemy. We need to look within and examine our own intolerance before we can communicate honestly.

It's not easy to face up to one's imperfections, but I believe most of us can do it, especially if our goal is to reach a new level of understanding in our families and in society.

SEEK THE OTHER PERSON'S POINT OF VIEW

Now that you've spent some time looking at your underlying feelings about people who strongly disagree with you, let's take a moment to work out what the other person holds dear. Step two is to try to see the religious dispute in your family from the other person's perspective.

Imagine that you went to sleep and woke up the next morning with the exact life history, values and beliefs of the family member who has been getting on your nerves about religion. Imagine that you temporarily have become that person. Try to understand why he or she feels so passionately about the viewpoint that has been upsetting you. To gain important insights that might help to improve communication in your family, ask yourself:

- How does this person justify his beliefs?
- What has this person studied, learned or experienced that may have resulted in her holding this belief?
- To whom does this person feel loyal or connected to while holding this view?
- What positive outcome does this person think will happen if others – if you – were to hold the same view?
- What does this other person believe is the deeper issue that this particular belief or practice makes sense of?

Trying to understand the perspective of another person is not easy, but it's essential if you're going to have a successful breakthrough conversation with your relation who holds an opposing religious (or anti-religious) viewpoint. It is a key step towards reducing friction and rebuilding a connection.

Quite often what happens at this point is that even though you disagree with the other person about certain issues, you might be able to agree about some underlying values. To illustrate what I mean, imagine two family members arguing about whether to smack a child. One person might say it's a traditional religious teaching that to spare the rod is to spoil the child, while the other person might say that spankings are abusive or counterproductive. It looks as if the two family members disagree.

But if you go deeper, you may see that both family members want to bring up a healthy child who feels loved, who can live within reasonable limits and who shows a healthy degree of self-discipline. At that point of agreement, the two family members can brainstorm and discuss different ways of imparting love and sensible boundaries to a child. Instead of arguing or resenting each other, the two could become allies in developing healthy ways of rearing responsible children.

Or if two family members are clashing about their different concepts of God or spiritual practice, they could use this bonding process to stop belittling each other's viewpoints and instead realize that both of their beliefs (or one's nonbelief) come from intelligent minds trying to make sense of one of life's great mysteries. It need not be a fight, but could be a thoughtful conversation about how humbling and profound it is trying to understand the mysterious creative force that connects all of us.

Ending a painful power struggle

If you decide that you are serious about transforming a religious clash into a caring and productive conversation, you may be surprised at how quickly it can reduce the tension between you and the family members whose beliefs you have found so frustrating. For example, in my own family there was an ongoing struggle that caused a lot of hurt feelings. Specifically, my wife Linda and I each year would attend important services at a progressive synagogue that she and I have been part of for many years. My wife's parents were very upset because they wanted us to join them at their own, more traditional congregation, where the services are conducted almost entirely in rapidly spoken Hebrew.

For several years my wife and I resented their 'interference'. Her parents were set in their ways and unwilling to let us go to our own services without bombarding us with angry comments and guilt-inducing remarks. On several occasions, the phone calls and dinner table arguments with her parents were so upsetting that my wife and her mother were both reduced to tears.

Then, a few years ago, my wife and I did the exercise described above. Imagining ourselves to be her parents, we asked each other, 'What is the deeper reason they argue so strongly for attending their services? What positive outcome do they hope for?'

We realized that her parents see the services from a very different perspective from ours. For us, a 'meaningful' and 'accessible' service is a top priority. But for her parents and many other people, being together as a unified family is the top priority. Being in a traditional setting, where the prayer structure and music are consistent and familiar, is also very important to them.

As a result of taking seriously her parents' perspective, we could see that family closeness is not so terrible; in fact, it's a quite reasonable thing to want. For the first time, we could understand that my wife's parents' desire for family togetherness and our desire for 'meaningful' worship *both* need to be respected.

An internal shift was beginning to happen for both Linda and me – we no longer saw the issue as who was right and who was wrong. Both sides had a legitimate case. Each year from then on, we experimented with different solutions. One year we went to both our synagogue and her parents' congregation for different services. One year Linda and I took our alternative prayer book and read it silently during the more traditional service at my in-laws' synagogue. One year we invited my wife's parents to come to the service at our synagogue and achieved a surprisingly strong sense of family closeness in a new setting. One year my wife and I abandoned our preference for an innovative service and became fully immersed in the beauty and majesty of her parents' services. There were still some moments when I was uncomfortable with the traditional approach, but it was a wonderfully inspiring service in many ways.

'I have also felt deeply moved at times'
I was thinking about the painful clashes that had happened with my wife's parents during the session at my clinic when Susan and Bill were anticipating the religious battles that might take place with their future daughter-in-law Claire. You will recall that Susan and Bill were feeling somewhat appalled at the idea of their son marrying someone whose religious beliefs were significantly different from their own. Yet a similar breakthrough happened for Susan and Bill when they imagined having Claire's perspective for a moment.

As Bill explained, 'It was hard at first to do the questions you set us for homework, to imagine ourselves believing and practising religion the way Claire does. I had grown up so alienated from formal organized religion that I had trouble putting myself in Claire's shoes. But then Susan and I decided to talk to Evan about what he finds so admirable and interesting about Claire's strong faith and values.'

Bill continued, 'We learned in just one phone call that Claire's passionate beliefs are a crucial part of why Evan is so attracted to her. According to Evan, "Claire is not someone who can be conned or manipulated by a trend or a whim." He told us how Claire is an extremely good person at her very core, and her religious involvement is an important factor in what keeps her so strong and centred.'

Susan added, 'I had always felt somewhat sceptical about Claire going to her Pentecostal church service where lots of people raise their hands and say the spirit is moving them. But then Evan told us how those services moved him to tears. Suddenly, Claire's religious intensity began to make sense. I have also felt deeply moved by a spiritual service with passionate music. But I realized that for most of my life I've felt somewhat inhibited about admitting too openly or loudly that life is a miracle and that the ultimate source of life is truly magnificent. I've always practised religion in a fairly restrained and cautious way. So for a moment, I could appreciate that Claire loves life and God so much that she's willing to say it out loud in a lively way. Maybe Claire's openness might open me up a bit, too.'

Bill and Susan both said that they still disagree with Claire on certain political and social issues. But they admitted for the first time, 'If Claire is able to transmit a joy for life and God, as well as a strong sense of compassionate values to our grandchildren, then that won't be a bad thing.' For the first time since Evan met Claire, Evan's parents Susan and Bill were beginning to see Claire as a complex human being with great strengths. They were beginning to imagine a healthy debate instead of a heated battle or a cold war with Claire about their differing ideas on how to bring up ethical children.

RESPECT EACH OTHER'S SIMILARITIES AND DIFFERENCES

The third and final step of the process is the most risky and the most powerful for building bridges in your family. Step three involves sitting down for a creative brainstorming session with the family member for whom you have felt ideological contempt or religious friction. During this brainstorming session, you and the other person are to come up with one or more realistic answers to the following questions:

- Is there a book, an activity or a one-off event that you would be willing to experience with an open mind in order to understand more deeply the path this other person is on?

- Is there a book, an activity, or a one-off event *you would like the other person* to experience with an open mind in order to understand more deeply the path you are on?

- Are there any activities, values or basic principles that you and the other person *do* agree on?

- Are there activities, values or basic principles that you and the other person absolutely *don't* agree on and that you will probably have to accept?

Agreeing to disagree – compassionately

Sitting down and having a calm and productive conversation with this other person about what you can do to learn more about each other might not be easy. You might require a counsellor, friend, mediator or clergy member to be there to support your efforts and to make sure you both treat each other with respect. Remember, you are not trying to convert one another – your goal is simply to learn a little more about the complexity and depth of why you both hold such different viewpoints.

'It was like going on a first date'

When Bill and Susan sat down with Evan and Claire to talk about ways to bridge their differences, all four were nervous.

Susan recalled, 'It was like going on a first date with someone. I felt extremely vulnerable and uncomfortable.'

But then Bill opened the discussion by saying, 'Our goal is to open a debate that hopefully will last for many years, no matter what tensions arise in our family. We'll always want the communication to be caring and respectful between the four of us. Even when we disagree with each other about important issues, it would be great if we could still have mutual respect for each other's beliefs.'

That opening statement reduced the tension and set the tone for what turned into a fascinating brainstorming session. As a result of their initial session, Susan, Bill, Evan and Claire came up with a list of ways to address the four issues listed above. Over the next few months they tested out a few of these ideas.

Susan and Bill attended a few Sunday services at Claire's church. According to Bill, 'I still found myself a bit reserved, but I could see that Susan was deeply moved by the sincerity of Claire's close friends at church and the way they celebrate life and spirituality. Susan said at one point in the service, "I wish I had grown up in a congregation with this much closeness and life."'

Claire agreed to come to an all-day workshop on spirituality and environmental issues at Susan's church. Claire also joined Susan at a lunch where she met Susan's minister, who is a highly respected spokesman for various liberal causes. According to Claire, 'I loved the workshop but I must admit that I didn't agree with everything the minister said at the lunch. But I could see we came from similar places in trying to bring our love for God into the world.'

Evan and Claire made a promise to Susan and Bill that they would always teach their future children how both sides of an issue can have an ethical and compassionate basis. They promised that even when they disagreed with Susan and Bill's position, they would explain both viewpoints to their children and treat both sides with respect. For instance, Claire told her future in-laws, 'I don't think you and I will ever agree about abortion, but I will always respect the fact that we simply have different ways of doing what we think is for the best. I believe it's healthy that our children will see us showing how family members can agree to disagree lovingly.'

You may find that in your own family, the first session is a lot less smooth or productive than what happened for Susan and Bill. But don't give up. In each of our families, there is always the possibility that even the most rigid and dogmatic individual will see that you are willing to respect the depth of their beliefs, even if you disagree respectfully with them. If this family member feels understood and respected by you, there is a good chance that sooner or later this person will start to recognize that you, too, have a legitimate basis for your own beliefs and opinions.

I can't predict whether there will be a breakthrough regarding the religious warfare in your particular family. But I have seen from experience that in most cases when you use this three-step process to work through your own judgments and intolerance, amazing kinds of bridge building can occur.

Our world is currently facing a dangerously high level of intolerance between religions and within varying denominations of each religious tradition. Our families, our schools, our neighbourhoods and our society need to find creative solutions in which divergent views can co-exist peacefully. How well we communicate with our own family members is the beginning of this search for mutual respect and co-existence. Good luck!

CHAPTER FIVE

HOW TO RESOLVE FAMILY BATTLES ABOUT FOOD, WEIGHT, CLOTHES AND APPEARANCE

One of the great ironies of life is that most people say hurtful things to their loved ones that they would never say to a stranger or even to an enemy. To a stranger walking down the street, one would never say, 'You're looking a little fat' or 'I don't think that colour suits you.' Nor would a polite person say to a stranger, 'Where did you get that awful haircut?' or 'Is that a cold sore on your lip?' Yet quite often you will hear family members say these and other critical or invasive things to each other, often under the guise of 'I was just trying to be helpful.'

If this never happens in your family, then count yourself among the lucky few. In the vast majority of families it's hard to get through a family event without one or more relatives saying something highly personal that hits home in someone's most vulnerable spot. At the supposedly happiest times of the year, thousands of us turn up at family gatherings hoping to have a good time, only to find ourselves amazed once again at some of the insensitive things that come out of people's mouths.

At your own family get-togethers, are there one or more relatives who say hurtful things under the guise of being helpful?

- 'You seem to have put on a few pounds.'
- 'Are you *really* going to wear that?'
- 'Do have some more. I didn't cook all day for nothing.'
- 'Are you *sure* you should be eating that?'
- 'You eat like a bird. Are you anorexic?'
- 'I see it's been a while since you had your roots done.'
- 'You don't look well, darling.'
- 'You shouldn't smile like that. It gives you wrinkles.'
- 'Stand up straight. You don't want to look like a failure, do you?'
- 'Forget about your diet. This is a special occasion. Have some pudding.'
- 'That outfit makes you look tarty.'
- 'Are you getting a spot on your nose?'
- 'Oh, do try some meat. You're not really a vegetarian.'
- 'Unfortunately, you've got your father's nose.'
- 'You're as thin as a rake. We've got to fatten you up.'

What can you do – if anything – to prevent such comments from being made in the future?

If you were to confront your most difficult relative about why he is trying to hurt you with his critical remarks, he would probably look at you as if you were mad. 'I'm not trying to hurt you,' he is likely to say. 'I'm trying to help.' Just as a parent reaches over and cuts up solid food in order to help a two-year-old eat her dinner, so your relatives think they are doing you a favour when they comment on your appearance. The big difference is that you are no longer two years old and there's something bizarre about a relative who can't stop trying to control your eating habits, choice of clothes and other personal matters.

As a therapist who has witnessed hundreds of families in my clinic arguing about food, clothes, weight and appearance, I can offer a few psychological reasons why 'helpful' relatives can't seem to stop themselves from saying invasive and hurtful things to the person they think they are helping. I've found that in most cases, the person giving advice is knowingly or unknowingly trying to pass on a painful family legacy about food or appearance that he or she inherited in the past.

What do I mean by a 'painful family legacy?' For one of my clients, it was simply that her overweight grandfather, who died from blocked arteries, was always saying, '*Mangia, mangia* – eat, eat!' This pressure to overeat at every meal then got passed down to my client's parents, who attempted to pass on the legacy by always urging her to eat more. Even if she was absolutely full or on a diet, her relatives felt compelled to push her to '*Mangia, mangia*, eat, eat, don't stop until you can barely stand up.' As this client told me during a counselling session, 'I love my family, but they are so intent on eating vast quantities of food it drives me mad.'

Or, the painful family legacy might be that someone told your grandmother at least a thousand times that she should lose a few pounds. Then your grandmother told your mother at least five hundred times that *she* should lose a few pounds. In turn, your mother has said to you at least three hundred times that you should lose a few pounds. This painful legacy about never being thin enough gets passed down from one generation to the next. At every family gathering, the pressure to 'lose a few pounds' becomes as crucial to the meal as a napkin or a fork.

UNDERSTANDING AND RESPONDING TO INVASIVE COMMENTS

The next time a family member gives you unsolicited advice or criticism about your weight or appearance, what will you do? Will you let it creep into your mind and make you insecure? Will you blow up in an angry outburst? Will you pretend it doesn't hurt you, when in fact it does?

To help you resolve what has been irritating you for so many years, consider the following situations to give you ideas about what you can do to respond more effectively to family pressures over such personal matters as weight and appearance. As you read the following four problems, notice which characters resemble the ones in your own family.

Problem one: a vain relative wants you to be obsessed with your looks

I once counselled a very handsome actor who dreaded family gatherings because his good-looking mother was endlessly critical of every minor physical imperfection her son had. According to this actor, 'My mother has spent her entire life using her good looks to her advantage, so she's always commenting on what I wear, telling me how to cure my imperfections, and how I should mix only with certain kinds of people. It's suffocating to be monitored and criticized by her year after year. Now she's trying to persuade me to have Botox injections so I won't have any wrinkles. She's so terrified of losing her own good looks, that that fear gets transferred to me whenever we're together.'

If one of your family members has a history of using her looks to get others to comply with her wishes, of course this person will want you to use the same tactics. This person feels compelled to give you endless unsolicited advice about how to look right, dress well and move properly in order to win friends and influence people. Or you may have found that this person is constantly badgering you with comments about your physical imperfections, hoping to inspire you to be as vigilant about your appearance as she is.

Because this family member is obsessed with appearance, you probably can't stop her from wanting to make suggestions about your looks. But you *can* ask yourself the following question. 'Do I want to be as obsessed as this family member, or do I want to relax about my looks so that my other positive features will be noticed?'

It's difficult to change the psyche of your family members, but you can make sure that you are in charge of your own life and your own sense of self-worth. The next time you are face-to-face with a vain member of your family, you may want to say to yourself silently, "Thank goodness I don't spend every waking moment as self-conscious as this person. Thank goodness I am able to keep my own self-criticism under control.'

Problem two: a relative is terrified you might suffer rejection

I once counselled a highly intelligent woman whose grandmother and mother had told her repeatedly that she needed to lose weight, change her hair, wear different clothes and put on more make-up if she was ever going to be happy in life. Ironically, this woman was a basically happy person, except when she was reeling from the insecurities about weight and appearance heaped on her by her mother and grandmother.

She told me during a counselling session, 'For my mother and my grandmother, there was a history of not getting accepted in the right social circles because of their plain looks. They also found it hard to find a husband, and in my mother's case to keep a husband. So they've tried to teach me over and over again that unless I do something to dramatically change my looks, my life will be spoiled. I try to ignore them, but I must admit it sometimes makes me unsure of myself both in social situations and sexually with my husband. My husband insists he finds me attractive, but sometimes when we're starting to get intimate I worry whether he really would prefer someone prettier. I wish I could just relax and not be so anxious about my appearance, but I still hear the warnings of my mother and my grandmother, which make me wonder whether one day I'll be sorry.'

If insecurities about looks and appearance have been programmed into your mind by insecure parents, siblings, grandparents, aunts, uncles or cousins, I strongly urge you to consider counselling to regain a truer sense of your self-worth, your attractiveness and your purpose in life. I have found repeatedly that when men and women directly address their physical insecurities in counselling, they almost always make significant progress.

But what can you say to yourself *right now* if a family member is criticizing your appearance? As in the first dilemma, you can't stop a relative from being insecure about her looks, but you can change the way you respond to her critical remarks. Instead of believing that she is talking about you and your life, you need to realize that most of the time when she comments about your weight or appearance she is simply releasing her own inner pain. You can empathise, but please remember that your looks and your attractiveness are an entirely different matter from hers.

Next time you hear one of your relatives trying to resolve his or her own insecurities by commenting on your appearance, you might want to say silently to yourself, 'Nice try, but I'm not travelling down that negative road with you. My job is to remember I'm an attractive human being, even when I'm bombarded by your poisonous comments.'

Or you can say to yourself, 'This is a test. Am I going to let this person define who I am, or am I going to recognize this person is a lot more uncomfortable with his or her looks than I'll ever be?'

Problem three: an overweight relative gives you dieting advice

At a family dinner you might hear someone with a lifelong eating compulsion or a history of failed diets making invasive remarks in order to 'help' someone else at the table. The advice-giving person has an endless supply of opinions she thinks you need to hear about what to eat and what not to eat. It's as though the more she focuses on *your* eating habits, the less she feels inadequate about her own.

At such moments, you may want to use your sense of ironic humour to say silently to yourself, 'I'm so glad this person is experiencing some relief from her self-loathing. How wonderful that I can be of service. Now I just need to make sure that I don't make the same mistake and start giving advice to someone else about what they should or shouldn't eat.'

You might also need to say something directly to this person to get them to stop focusing on you and your eating habits. One response that usually works is to say in a calm voice, 'You're probably right. I'll think about your ideas. But for now, let's talk about something else besides food and diets.' 80 per cent of the time, this kind of non-confrontational, conciliatory line will get you out of the situation.

But if your beloved relative happens to be one of the obsessive 20 per cent who simply can't stop assaulting others with advice about food, you might need a stronger response. You might want to say in a calm but firm voice, 'I appreciate that you're trying to be helpful, but I don't want to hear one more word about food or diet.' In most cases, the invasive person will back off and the conversation can move on to some other topic.

If you're concerned, however, that this response might start a nuclear war in your nuclear family, you don't need to say it. Instead, you might want to prepare the ground in advance and ask one of your other family members to say it for you. In a phone call a few days before the family meal, ask one or two of your family members for help. 'When Aunt Sophie starts talking about what I should eat or not eat, could you say to her, "That's enough. No more comments about weight or diets."'

In most cases, if you prepare ahead of time to have at least one or two family members ready to step in for you, you can stop even the most invasive relatives from ruining your meal. You'd be amazed at how just a few well-chosen words from the right ally can stop even a stampeding rhinoceros in its tracks.

'It's impossible just to enjoy a meal'
Claudia is a recent client who told me, 'My family dinners are a nightmare. I try not to be too obsessed about my weight, but I've got one aunt who lectures about how many calories there are in everything you're eating, and she preaches constantly about which foods have too much cholesterol. I've got an uncle who also likes to manage what everyone is eating and tells us repeatedly how he lost forty pounds once with

Weight Watchers. I've got a younger step-sister from my father's new family who has a perfect body and loves to criticize the rest of us for having the "lack of willpower" that she thinks is the reason why we bigger-boned women don't look like her. My father adores this flirtatious little step-sister and it drives me round the bend. Every meal in our family involves people taking potshots at one another about how we're not quite living up to our diets and food plans. It's impossible just to enjoy a meal.'

When I asked Claudia if she would be willing to speak up and tell her relatives that she wanted to focus on something other than food, she started to laugh. 'Some hope. They would turn on me in a flash and make the rest of the meal about *my* physical imperfections.'

So I asked Claudia, 'Is there anyone else in your family who could be your ally and insist that the conversation has to stop being just about food and weight?' Claudia thought for a moment, and said, 'You know who's got that kind of clout in my family? My grandfather has. And I'm his favourite.'

Before the next family gathering, Claudia asked her grandfather if he would be willing to speak up and stop the discussion from focusing on food and diets for the umpteenth year in a row. Her grandfather replied, 'I'd love to be the one to shut them up.'

A few days later, at the family gathering, Claudia was starting to eat her main course when her calorie-counting aunt began to preach – again. Within seconds, the respected grandfather tapped his spoon on a glass of wine and announced, 'Excuse me, there's a new rule I'd like to propose. No more talking about diets, calories or cholesterol. No more giving each other advice about losing weight. Let's talk about life and adventures and what's going on for each of us. Let's

make this an enjoyable meal.' As Claudia described, 'It was
spooky – at first there was complete silence. If we couldn't
obsess about food, then what else was there to talk about?
But then my cousin, who lives abroad, asked us to talk about
the most challenging and the most satisfying things in each of
our lives since we were together last year. It turned into a fascinating discussion. For the first time ever, I ate a relaxed meal
with my extended family.'

Problem four: a relative equates food with love

In nearly every family I've counselled over the years, I've
noticed there is at least one person who mixes up food with
love. It might be someone who always cooks far too much
food and feels unloved when there is some left over. Or it
might be someone who gets hurt or offended if someone
turns up at a family meal on a restrictive diet or special food
programme. Instead of supporting your healthy habits, this
person feels hurt that you aren't wolfing down every morsel
that's been lovingly cooked for you. She can't seem to understand that taking care of yourself by not eating certain foods
might be a good thing. This food-obsessed person takes it personally when you don't overeat. 'You don't appreciate it,' she
might think or say; 'You don't really love me.'

If someone in your family hounds you to eat loads of
food to prove your love for her, have a heart-to-heart talk
with her. Let your insecure relative know that you do love
her. Explain how much you wish you could eat every delicious bite that's been lovingly prepared. Remind her how
much you appreciate all the planning, hard work and caring
that go into the entire meal. Then carefully explain to her
what you will be able to eat or not eat at the next family

gathering. Treat her like a special co-conspirator helping you on a secret mission. The mission is that you and she are going to design a meal that combines both love and food, but with sensible quantities and foods that you can manage to eat.

In fact, brainstorming ahead of time with the host or menu planner for a family gathering is crucial for anyone on a restrictive diet, or who has a medical need to avoid certain foods, a vegetarian lifestyle or food allergies that need to be taken seriously. Especially when your relatives are likely to equate uneaten food with unrequited love, you will need to address these concerns well ahead of time. By having a conversation a few weeks before a family event, you can make sure your family gatherings and meals will not be a power struggle or a source of guilt feelings.

In this pre-event planning phone call or visit, simply say to your relative who wants to feel appreciated, 'I know that you care about everyone's well-being, so let's see what we can make or what I can bring. I don't want to put you to any trouble. I want you to know how much I appreciate all the care and love you put into these events but I need you to help me by supporting the special diet I'm on.' Then work together to develop a specific plan for what the other person will make that you can eat, or what you can bring so that there will be the right foods for your diet.

In most cases, your 'I need you to eat to prove your love' family member will co-operate if she or he gets treated gently and honestly far enough in advance of the family gathering. But in some cases, there are prickly, self-centred or narcissistic family members who will be hurt or offended even by this kind of considerate pre-planning effort. Take, for example, the following scenario.

'Would it kill you just to eat what someone serves you?'
Barry has severe food allergies and can't eat dairy products.
He also has a mother-in-law who is an amazing gourmet cook
and who feels terribly hurt whenever he turns down any of
her elegant treats that almost always have rich creamy sauces
or cheesy fillings. Several times Barry's mother-in-law has
commented, 'Barry, why aren't you eating? Don't you like my
cooking?' Barry has tried to explain each time that he's aller-
gic to dairy products. Yet each time his mother-in-law looks
hurt or rejected. Barry feels guilty for hurting his mother-in-
law, and Barry's wife feels caught in the middle.

When I explained to Barry the technique of a proactive
phone call for menu planning, he liked the idea. He then
called his mother-in-law and tried to discuss a sensible plan
for the next family party. He didn't want to inconvenience his
wife's mother. So he offered to bring a few casseroles that
worked with his restrictive diet.

Barry's mother-in-law was horrified. She phoned Barry's
wife and cried into the phone, 'I don't understand why your
husband hates me so much. I try so hard to please everyone
and then he goes and slaps me in the face like this.'

'What happened, Mum?' Barry's wife asked.

'Your husband wants to bring some bland tofu dish to
my dinner party. That would be so humiliating. Why can't
your generation be a little less selfish and just compromise
once in a while? What is it with your me-me-me attitude?
Would it kill you just to eat what someone serves you?'

Barry's wife replied, 'I've told you he gets severe intesti-
nal flare-ups if he eats dairy products.'

Her mother was quiet for a moment, and then said, 'You
don't know how hard I try to make these dinners special.
Why do you make it so difficult?'

Clearly, Barry and his wife were dealing with someone who has a serious case of confusing food and love. Like many of our relatives who think they are being caring when they say 'Eat, eat, eat,' Barry's mother-in-law was more concerned with her own fragile ego than with Barry's health or well-being.

So I suggested to Barry, 'Rather than fighting with your insecure mother-in-law about food or control, give her a chance to be a heroine. What works best with a fragile or self-centred family member who feels betrayed when you stand up for your needs is to appeal to their shaky sense of self-esteem and let them know you are not a threat. Tell her what an amazing cook she is and ask her if she'd be willing to teach the two of you to make a gourmet dish that doesn't contain any dairy products. You might want to give her a special cookery book that uses soya or rice products that you can eat safely. Let her know that you both think she's a marvellous hostess and that she's the only person creative enough to make one of these recipes both delicious and sophisticated.'

That was the beginning of a breakthrough in Barry's struggles with his mother-in-law. As he told me a few days after the dinner party, 'My mother-in-law, my wife and I had a unique cooking session a few days before the event. My wife and I had brought a few recipes that avoided cheese, milk and cream, but my mother-in-law was worried that these tofu and veggie dishes were far too boring. So she gave us a lesson on how to make the taste and the presentation as elegant as the rest of her meal would be. She was so proud of herself. Not only was she finally able to get me to eat her cooking, but for the first time ever she had got her daughter to take a gourmet cooking lesson from her. On the night of the family party, the three of us were like allies or co-conspirators. We had developed in secret a creative way to make healthy food taste delicious.'

Each of our families has a slightly different version of the conflict over food and appearance. As you think about your own family, remember that the goal is not to prove who's right and who's wrong about food preferences or standards of appearance. Instead, the goal is to find a creative way to become allies in putting together a family event that everyone can enjoy. As Barry discovered with his mother-in-law, if you let your difficult relative be the hero or heroine of the story, you will usually find that you can bring out the best in someone who for too long has been your worst adversary.

IS IT EVER APPROPRIATE FOR FAMILY MEMBERS TO GIVE ADVICE?

While I have found that the vast majority of family members do not enjoy receiving advice from one another, there are a few exceptions. I've seen instances when a family member turns to a relative and says, 'I've always been impressed by how well you dress [or how you look, wear make-up, style your hair, stay slim or something similar]. Would you be willing to share your secrets?' If that happens, feel flattered by the compliment and by all means reveal your best tips.

The fine art of giving advice

But before you rush into a situation and risk assaulting family members with unsolicited advice or criticism, here are a few ground rules for giving advice properly.

Don't take your own issues out on others. Before giving anyone advice, ask yourself first if you are in any way telling someone else to do what you yourself have had trouble doing. For instance, rather than saying, 'Don't eat that fattening pudding,' look at your own struggle to refrain from high-calorie or unhealthy foods. Then wait until the other person directly asks for help on how to lose weight before offering him or her any advice.

Avoid shaming anyone. When giving advice, it's best to avoid making someone's weight or appearance the topic of conversation at a family meal. Instead, talk to the person in private and avoid embarrassing them. In most spiritual and religious traditions as well as in proper etiquette, it's recommended that you give helpful feedback one-to-one in a respectful way and never allow anyone's vulnerability to be exploited in idle conversation. Remember, the best way to help loved ones change for the better is *not* to undermine their self-confidence but to let them know you are rooting for them as they follow their own goals.

Focus on what someone can change and don't criticize what he cannot. Make sure any advice you offer is aimed at improving this person's changeable behaviours and avoid any attacks on his or her character or any irreversible physical or emotional traits. Before you open your mouth, ask yourself, 'Am I commenting on this person's basic body type or basic personality structure, which can't be changed? Or am I commenting on a specific behaviour that this person says he or she wants to change with help from the rest of us?' Most importantly, you need to ask yourself, 'Am I building on what this person has said she wants to achieve, or am I unrealistically asking her to become an entirely different person with cruel comments like "Why can't you be like so and so?"'

'You know what your problem is?'
Nigel's case is a good illustration of the difference between insulting, harmful advice and truly helpful advice. A 30-year-old middle manager for a high-tech company, Nigel had been

coming to therapy for a few weeks to talk about the tensions in his family, and to see if he could make this Christmas more enjoyable.

According to Nigel, 'In my family, people have no tact at all when it comes to commenting on your weight or your looks. For instance, my younger brother Rick is a talented recent architecture graduate, but he hasn't been able to find a job yet. So last month at a birthday dinner at a restaurant, my older sister Angela said, "Rick, you know what your problem is? Your hair looks like shit and you dress like a 1990s grunge fan queuing for Nirvana tickets. Your clothes and your hair say to every prospective employer, 'Don't employ me! I'm a slacker'."'

Nigel recalled, 'There was some truth in what Angela was saying, but the Olympic judges wouldn't give her high marks for presentation. You could see Rick squirming, feeling awful that he'd been very close at several interviews to getting a good job, but never quite been the one selected. Then my mother started defending Rick and telling Angela that she was being rude. So of course Angela shouted, 'But can't you see he looks like a loser!' Rick stormed out of the restaurant and drove home. By the time my sister Wendy's birthday cake arrived, my mother was in tears and Angela was defending herself, saying, "What? Don't look at me. I was just trying to be helpful."'

Does this sound at all familiar? Do you also have a family where people give each other harsh criticism or advice in public and it degenerates into a nasty scene? Do you have good intentions to help each other, but often end up with hurt feelings?

To change the family pattern that had been causing pain for as long as Nigel could remember, we discussed the three ground rules listed above. Could Nigel talk to Rick one-to-one instead of in front of the whole family? Could he make his comments in a kind way? And could he focus on what Rick wanted to improve about himself rather than asking him to be someone else?

Finding the right words and tone of voice to help a family member who really needs advice is crucial in many families. We all want to help the people we love. But even the slightest hint of condescension or disrespect can turn your well-intentioned advice into yet another personality clash or ugly scene.

Nigel commented to me a few days before the next family gathering, 'I think my brother Rick does want and need some advice about how to dress more like an architect and less like a grungy student. But how do I give him advice without pissing him off or sounding like Angela?'

After a counselling session in which Nigel practised a few ways of expressing his advice, here's what happened.

At a family lunch a few days later, everyone was watching television and having drinks. Knowing there was at least an hour until food was going to be served, Nigel asked Rick to go for a walk and took the opportunity to tell him, 'I think you're extremely well-qualified to get a great job. But can I offer you a few suggestions about how to make the interviews more successful? If I promise not to push anything down your throat or sound like Angela, would you be prepared to throw around some ideas to boost your odds at an interview?'

Rick replied, 'How do I know you're not going to be a jerk like Angela?'

Nigel smiled and said, 'I can't guarantee not to say anything stupid. But I promise to treat you with a lot more respect than you usually get in this family.'

That seemed to relax Rick, and the brothers spent half an hour discussing how to look, act and respond to tough questions in an interview. They focused on a few specific interviewing outfits, hair styles and tones of voice that could balance Rick's desire for informality along with a clear impression of his maturity and professionalism.

Nigel told me a week later, 'This was a breakthrough because Rick was finally willing to take charge of his appearance and stop shooting himself in the foot by being too informal. But it was also a breakthrough because it was the first time I can remember two people stepping outside the family lunacy and talking to each other with real warmth and compassion.'

Almost six weeks after the holiday talk with Nigel, Rick received a job offer from a good architecture practice. Rick called Nigel and said, 'It was the best interview I'd ever done, in part because of your help.'

As Nigel told me during his final counselling session a few weeks later, 'That one conversation with Rick was still the exception. My family continues to be brutal and invasive in the way they talk about each other's weight and appearance. But this gave me hope that in future there will be a few more exceptions to the family rule. I hope with each passing year there will be more chances to help each other without hurting one another. Even if my family is still pretty much the same, there will be enough successes to let me know that a few of us can come through for each other.'

The next time you are with your extended family, notice the way people inadvertently hurt one another with their harsh comments about food, weight and looks. Then resolve to do whatever you can to increase, even in the smallest way, the level of respect and caring in your family. It may seem like a small shift, but it can make a huge difference.

CHAPTER SIX

WHY FAMILIES ARE SENSITIVE ABOUT MONEY, STATUS AND COMPETITION

(AND WHAT YOU CAN DO ABOUT IT)

Where do you fit in as a member of your family? Are you the 'golden one' who people look up to and consider a success? Are you the 'troublemaker' or 'rebel' who faces a lot of disapproval or criticism from your relatives? Are you the 'under-appreciated, hard-working, behind-the-scenes person' who takes care of details while others enjoy the spotlight and the praise? Are you one of the decision makers in your extended family, or are you often left out of crucial plans or conversations?

Whether our relatives admit it or not, every family has members who rank highly and others who get ignored or overlooked. And most people don't realize just how much their place in the pecking order has to do with money, status and other comparisons that often cause hurt feelings and tensions between relatives.

I wish this were not the case – I wish that each family member could be treated as a unique individual with equal value and worth. But in fact I've found that there is favouritism and unequal treatment in nearly every one of the thousands of families I've seen over the years.

Take, for example, your own family:

> Is there someone in your immediate or extended family who is given more respect or clout than you think he deserves, but because he has lots of money or status the family puts him on a pedestal and usually lets him have his way?

> Is there someone in your immediate or extended family who has less status or influence than you think is fair, but because she is broke the family treats her like a black sheep, a nonentity or a disappointment?

> Do you have an affluent or classy relative in whose presence you sometimes feel belittled or self-conscious? Do you compare your imperfect home, your imperfect furnishings, your imperfect car, your imperfect children and your imperfect career to hers?

> Is there a less affluent or less successful member of your family who occasionally looks at you with envy or resentment over what you have and what he wishes he had?

> Are there members of your family who went along with family expectations about which career or which kind of spouse to choose, while other family members have followed a different path that the family has trouble accepting?

> Are there some members of your family who aren't on speaking terms or who are distant from others

because of a financial disagreement that may go back many years (or even more than a generation)?

Does someone in your family dole out gifts, attention, financial assistance, praise and encouragement in unequal doses – favouring some individuals and neglecting others?

Does someone in your family favour one family member's children or grandchildren?

This chapter is not about how to make lots of money, or how to invest it. Instead, the next few pages will address a topic that causes significant amounts of emotional distance in nearly every family: how to deal with the painful comparisons your relatives may make between you and others. We will explore how to achieve balance and satisfaction in life, even if you come from a family that pressured you to pursue money and status above all else. And you'll find a few healthy ways to respond to the inevitable jealousies and rivalries that many families foster.

THE FUNNY THING ABOUT MONEY

One of the fascinating things that I've seen while counselling is that money is an equal opportunity neurosis-maker – it causes family tensions no matter how rich, poor or middle-class your background. For instance, I once counselled a woman who grew up extremely poor, and even though she was well-to-do for most of her life, those memories of growing up feeling inferior to her affluent cousins never left her. At the opposite extreme, I counselled a man who grew up extremely rich and spent his entire life insecure about the fact that his relatives all saw him as less of a man than his enormously successful father and grandfather. I also counselled a woman whose parents were quite affluent, but because they lived well into their nineties, this woman always felt like an heiress without an inheritance.

I have counselled numerous men and women who grew up in middle-class families where there was tremendous pressure from some relatives to make it and equal pressure from other relatives to 'stay as you are and don't become like the snobby rich lot'. There are other middle-class people whose relatives expected them to live as well or better than previous generations, but because of how expensive houses and other things are today, they feel like failures because they are having to live in less affluent circumstances than their parents. Despite being well-educated and working hard at good jobs, most middle-class people today feel unsure about whether they will ever be able to afford the kind of lifestyle their parents told them to expect.

Many people have mixed feelings about money and how it affects their relationships with their families. On the one hand, you want to have a comfortable life and make your family proud. On the other hand, you may have picked up subtle messages from certain relatives that if you focus too much on success or material comforts, they will resent you or feel alienated from you. Or you might find that your pursuit of financial success makes you too busy to find time for the family, who then feel slighted.

SORTING OUT WHAT YOU CAN AND CANNOT CONTROL

If you want to do something positive about the money and status issues in your family, you will first need to clarify what your relatives can change and what they are unable or unwilling to change. Here are some examples.

- You probably can't change the minds of those family members who have given you subtle or not-so-subtle messages that 'I'll love you more if you follow the lifestyle I've chosen for you.'
- You probably can't change the fact that some of your relatives are so focused on status or affluence that they have trouble seeing the humanity, the soul or the worth of people who don't care as much about status or affluence as they do.
- You probably can't change the fact that a few of your relatives are so insecure, wounded or driven to make up for the financial frustrations stemming from their childhood experiences that they have become judgmental, impatient or overbearing towards any family member who doesn't share their constant drive for success and status.
- You probably can't change the fact that you come from a family that sometimes sends contradictory messages, such as (on the one hand) 'don't be too concerned about money', and (on the other hand) 'whatever you've accomplished thus far is not enough.'
- You probably can't change the fact that there are members of your family who will resent you for making more money than them.

To accept that you probably cannot change many aspects of the money-and-status game in your family is not easy. For years you may have been hoping your relatives would become less rigid and more understanding about why you don't share their particular concerns about money and status. But let's face it: nearly all of our families to some extent have an element of idiocy about financial matters and what they think is 'the right way to live'. No matter how hard they try to deny it, you know that some of your relatives have strong opinions about what they – and what you – should value in life.

WHAT YOU CAN DO ABOUT MONEY AND STATUS

While there are many things that you can't change about your relatives' obsessions about money and status, there are some changes that you can make happen, even in the most status-conscious or materialistic family.

Identify pressures you grew up with

Most people are unaware of the subtle but painful money issues their relatives have passed on to them. As you think about the financial pressures, lifestyle pressures and mixed messages you've received from your family, it's crucial to take charge and tell the truth about the dilemmas and inse-curities that may have become part of your psyche. Only then will you be able to make healthy decisions about your own life.

'My father tried really hard to be a success'

For example, I once counselled a 46-year-old man, Dennis, who was referred to me for psychotherapy to help resolve his stress-related high blood-pressure, irritable bowel, and skin problems. The eldest son in a family of five adult children, Dennis told me during his first session, 'I don't really think I need to see a shrink. Basically, I've got my head screwed on. I just work too hard so I've got a lot of stress. But who doesn't work too hard these days?'

Like most people, Dennis was unaware of how his family had contributed to his high blood pressure, his digestive problems or his skin problems. In fact, like many loyal sons and daughters, Dennis felt somewhat guilty about questioning the way his parents pressured him as a child, and he was reluctant even to consider the possibility that his family was a partial cause of his stress.

Yet as we talked about his upbringing and his extended family today, an intriguing story emerged. According to Dennis, 'My grandfather was a well-to-do businessman in Asia before he had to flee with nothing but a small suitcase and only a small amount of money in his wallet. And when he got here, the money was missing. My grandfather never did make a satisfactory living. He was a brilliant man but he never worked out how business is done in the West.'

Dennis continued, 'My father tried really hard to be a success and make up for the frustrations my grandfather had experienced. As a result, my Dad worked such long hours that at the age of 44 he died from a heart attack and my two brothers and I went to work to support my Mum and our two younger sisters.'

Describing how his siblings responded to their father's death, Dennis said, 'All five of us were brought up in a household where making up for the financial hardships of the past was drilled into us. As a result, each of us has become extremely competitive and highly accomplished in our respective fields. Each of us also has a huge problem with stress – we all work so hard that none of us has been that successful at marriage or at bringing up children who don't resent us for never being around.' Dennis paused and looked

at me with a knowing expression on his face. He commented, 'I suppose maybe there is some connection
between the stressful way all of us live and the money pressures my parents and grandparents instilled in us.'

If your own family was anything like Dennis's family, they
probably didn't mean to tie you in knots over money and security. Rather, they were probably just trying to survive and to
make sure you didn't suffer the same hardships and disappointments they had faced. Yet the pressures and stresses of trying to make up for what your parents and grandparents never
quite achieved can weigh heavily on you and your loved ones.
That's why it's crucial to take time to uncover exactly what was
said or implied to you as a child. Only then can you begin to
reclaim your life and your emotional well-being.

To help sort out the ways in which your family has influenced your feelings about money and status, ask yourself the
following questions:

- What financial setbacks, daily pressures or painful
  disappointments did you and your parents face
  when you were growing up?
- What did your family teach you was the way to succeed or be happy in life, and what did they warn
  you was the way to fail or end up unhappy?
- Were there innocent or harmless things you were
  forbidden to do because they might make your family look bad to certain relatives or to the community?
- Did you or your family make any special effort to
  prove your status or worth?
- When you were growing up, which specific individuals were your relatives trying to impress? Who

were they afraid might judge them or exclude them? Who mattered most and who was less important in your immediate family, in your extended family, in your school and in the world at large?

– Have you ever been frustrated by not being able to afford something you wanted, or wished you could have the status or class of someone in your family, your school or your neighbourhood?

– Did you promise yourself as a child that you wouldn't repeat some of the mistakes you saw in your parents' lives? What are some of those mistakes?

By talking about these issues with a counsellor or friend, or by exploring these worries in a notebook or in letters or e-mails to a supportive friend or relative, you will have taken an important step towards deciding on your own adult values and lifestyle choices. You will be bringing your inner confusion or ambivalence about money to the surface so that you can examine it carefully and reasonably. Most people never take the time to uncover exactly what kinds of pressures, comparisons and competition their families forced upon them, but it's crucial to helping you stop being fuelled by shame and guilt, which can make you feel constantly anxious and filled with regret.

Once Dennis had explored several of the questions above, he looked sad as he told me, 'I never realized just how much I've been on automatic pilot trying to make up for what my grandfather and father never were able to accomplish. My life has been out of kilter for many years. My wife and children have been waiting for me to stop being such a workaholic. They've tried to tell me that I've become too obsessed with money and success, and that they just want me to be healthy

and live a longer life than my father did. Yet I've been resisting their advice and actually resenting them for not being
more supportive of my workaholic tendencies.'

To help Dennis deal more effectively with the pressures
of his upbringing and find ways to achieve greater balance in
his life now, we brainstormed and came up with three specific
things he was willing to do on a regular basis:

- First, he was willing to start each day with a short meditation session to help calm his anxious thoughts.
  Before his mind and his adrenalin started racing each
  morning, he would take a few moments to start the
  day with a sense of tranquillity and balance.

- Second, he was willing to spend a few minutes before
  lunch and before dinner taking a short break to listen
  to music, go for a walk or read some poetry. Instead of
  feeling caught on a treadmill, rushing to each meal
  only to gobble it down, Dennis used these relaxing
  moments to regain control over his chronic anxiety, his
  stress level and his digestive problems.

- Third, he was willing to set aside one day each week
  for enjoying pleasurable activities with his wife and
  children. Like many other workaholics I've counselled,
  Dennis had trouble at first setting aside this time for
  connecting with his loved ones, but once he got into
  the habit of doing it he made enormous progress in
  growing closer to his wife and their four children.

He told me during one of his final counselling sessions,
'I discovered that the best way of honouring my father and
grandfather was not to work myself into an early grave. The
best way of honouring what they went through is to become

the first one in our family to make a real connection with my wife and children. Even if I don't make as much money each year as my workaholic siblings, at least I will have lived a meaningful life.'

Please note that even though I have recommended to Dennis and to many others the importance of giving health and family a higher priority than money or status, I am not saying that people should neglect their work or their legitimate need for financial security. Seeking balance in life does not mean becoming oblivious to financial matters. In Dennis's case and in many other cases, the choice is not between being rich or poor. Rather, in most of our lives the choice is between overstressing ourselves in order to chase after more money and status than our parents had, versus choosing to live each day with a little more balance and a deeper commitment to health, family and friendships, and appreciating the beauty of art, nature, spirituality and helping others.

Only you and your loved ones know what kinds of imbalances are at work in your life. And only you can decide whether you want to explore the possibility of living a more balanced life than your family said was possible, while at the same time making enough money to support your commitments. Like Dennis, your goal might be to become the first branch on your family tree to achieve the emotional well-being that your parents, your grandparents and your other relatives were unable to find.

Make conscious choices about your self-worth

Maybe your relatives don't speak openly about money or finances but instead talk about what's right or wrong, what's in good taste or bad, what's valuable or useless and a waste of time. In many families the pressure isn't exactly about money but rather about what will make your relatives proud instead of treating you with disapproval or scorn.

As a child listening to all these opinions about who had class and who didn't, you probably sensed your family's expectations. You probably learned – too well – what kind of status, achievements or lifestyle choices would please them and which would make you a disappointment in their eyes.

In some families the pressure to live up to your relatives' expectations about status is a question of who you are going out with. Is she or he from a 'good family' or rather 'not what we had in mind for you'. Or the status issue in your particular family might have been about your differing tastes in furniture or home decorating, whether you belong to the right clubs, whether you drive a new BMW or an old Ford, or where your children go to school.

When you fall short of expectation, your status in the eyes of certain family members can drop. Then every family visit or phone call becomes another chance for your relatives to pressure you to start living up to their ideas about who they think you ought to be.

'I feared that my mother would never love me again'

One of my clients a few years ago was a well-mannered but somewhat unhappy 38-year-old woman named Caroline. According to Caroline, 'Status was never actually discussed in our family, but we knew from dozens of stories and examples mother told us that there were things we should never do or we would deeply hurt her. I remember having a boyfriend from the wrong sort of family and mother was as horrified as if I had become a prostitute or murderer.'

As in most families where there is a huge emphasis on what is acceptable and what is not, Caroline and her siblings felt a lot of shame and guilt. According to Caroline, 'My older sister and I tried to obey the rules, with mixed results. My older sister finished with the one man she ever really loved and married instead a well-respected investment banker from a 'good' family. But he turned out to be an alcoholic and a womanizer. My own well-bred husband was never actually unfaithful, but he turned out to be a cold and distant partner. Then recently my younger sister got engaged to someone whom the family sees as unacceptable, and that started an unspoken war between her and my relatives that has affected each family gathering since. It's not something we talk about openly; it's more an expression you see on my mother's face, a tightening of her lips and a frowning brow that says, "You've ruined everything." Or it's the way my aunt looks over her bifocals as she takes a deep breath that seems to say, "How could you do this to your mother after all she's done for you?" There's a lot of pressure to live up to our family's expectations.'

With Caroline and many other clients, I've found that if you clarify and make conscious choices about the many messages that you received as a child and young adult, you can dramatically improve not only your internal sense of well-being but the quality of your life. You can substantially reduce the guilt feelings.

For instance, when Caroline and I discussed who her family members were trying to impress and why they were so concerned about being acceptable, some important breakthroughs occurred. She recalled, 'My mother was always terrified of the rigid and opinionated members of her family, especially my aunt and my grandmother, who always made her feel bad if we children did anything messy, creative, spontaneous or childlike. My Mum was constantly trying to make sure we didn't make her look like a "permissive parent", which in our family was considered a sin. So she was really strict, and made us feel that if we ever did anything that embarrassed her in front of my aunt or my grandmother, then we were essentially breaking her heart. That's a lot of pressure to put on a child, and I remember crying my eyes out with guilt once when I accidentally spilled juice on my aunt's expensive rug. It felt like the end of the world, and I feared that my mother would never love me again.'

To help Caroline break out of the shame and guilt she had been living with for most of her life, we began to explore the pros and cons of seeking status and acceptability. First, we looked at her unhappy marriage, which Caroline admitted she had consented to in the first place to please her mother even though she herself had serious doubts. According to Caroline, 'My husband is a decent man and I don't want a divorce. But I don't know if I can live my whole life with so little warmth and affection.'

Hoping to improve the marriage rather than end it, she and her husband, Piers, went into couples counselling to work on the unhealthy roles and lack of warmth that had been hurting Caroline for several years. It took a few months, but Caroline found, 'Piers is still by nature a bit formal and reserved, but he's improved a lot as a husband because of our honest conversations and creative problem-solving in counselling. His listening skills and his ability to show empathy have become much stronger. We've also started to tackle some of our sexual problems. My mother and many of our relatives would be horrified if they knew that Piers and I have started taking a course in Tantric sex. Despite the fact that he and I were both brought up without much physical affection from our very proper families, we've warmed up our sex life quite a lot in the past few months.'

In addition to taking steps to improve her marriage, Caroline began to make conscious decisions about her choice of friends and activities. She explains, 'For years I subconsciously went along with my mother's values and had a very narrow social life as a result. But over the past year I've been breaking some of her rules. Every few weeks I've gone with new friends to dinner parties, cultural events, museums, films and dance clubs that would horrify Mum. It feels like at the age of 39 I'm finally starting to create my own life and make my own decisions. I was always a bit nervous that I'd embarrass my mother by living a little too freely. But the fact is, my mother is uncomfortable with just about everything I enjoy that is interesting or unusual. So why bother worrying that I might offend her sense of propriety? I've begun to realize she's in charge of her life and I'm the one who's in charge of mine.'

A word of warning. Caroline was able to break out of her shell safely and discreetly. But in some cases when people are brought up with very strict rules and a sense of guilt, they might burst out too clumsily and too impulsively as soon as the prison door is unlocked. I hope that you don't go out and do anything harmful to yourself or others in your quest to loosen the bonds. Remember, the goal is to build an adult life that is healthier and more alive than that of your anxious, status-obsessed family members. I wish you wisdom.

Stop competing with your relatives

I've found that one of the surest ways for a family to stunt someone's growth or crush someone's spirit is constantly to compare him or her to someone else in the family. You might recognize some of these.

- 'Why can't you be like your brother [or sister]?'
- 'So-and-so has a great job. Why can't you find one?'
- 'If you care about your father, you'll follow in his foot-steps.'
- 'You've got so much going for you. Why are you the only one still not married?'
- 'I never had this problem with any of your siblings. Why do you have to be so stubborn?'

In most families, there is at least one person who simply doesn't share the values and lifestyle decisions of the other family members. It's not about who's right or wrong but rather a question of moving beyond comparisons and competition.

If you happen to be the outcast in your family, the one who has a different notion of money and status than the other family members, please realize that you are not alone. Most creative people throughout history have found themselves alienated or scorned by their relatives. But what can you do to stay true to your unique way of living life? Or, if you are worried about someone else who is the black sheep or rebel in a family that simply cannot accept this person's way of life, how can you support this individual? How do you make sure he or she doesn't get crushed or excluded by the constant criticism from judgmental relatives?

'My family doesn't know what to do with me'
Lauren's case is a good example of someone who has been stung by too many comparisons with her relatives on the issues of money and status. Lauren is a bright and creative 32-year-old woman who told me in her first counselling session, 'My family doesn't know what to do with me. I'm a bundle of contradictions to them. On the one hand, I grew up with

a love for Celtic folk music, which I picked up from my maternal grandmother and which I studied at university. My interest is meaningless to my father, who's a self-made businessman. He thinks I'm a complete fool for pursuing my passion for music history and folk culture. My lack of money is a big joke to my older brother, who's a successful surgeon. I'm also having trouble with the constant judgments and advice from my younger sister, who has an affluent lifestyle and who's been divorced twice already from rich men whom she decided weren't making enough money to keep her happy.'

Lauren explains, 'You see, our family has a lot of emotional baggage about money and status. When I was a child, my Dad struggled to make ends meet. We lived in a very small house right on the edge of a very smart neighborhood. My brother, my sister and I knew quite clearly that we had a lot less money than most of the children at our highly competitive school. We also had less money than my rich cousins, who were always going on exotic holidays. In our family, my parents were extremely tight with money while my Dad's business was slowly growing. And they stayed tight with money after his business started to do well when I was at university.'

Lauren admits, 'I wish I could just be a full-time researcher of Irish music, storytelling and history. But even though my family thinks I'm oblivious to money, there's also a part of me that longs for financial security, a nice car that doesn't break down all the time and a decent house. I feel most at home when I'm wearing casual clothes and spending time with musicians, writers and teachers. But there's also a part of me that wishes I could have some of the creature comforts my brother and sister have. They live in gorgeous houses and I've got a tiny flat with wooden planks and bricks holding up all my books.'

Lauren told me during one of her sessions, 'I feel so divided between the suburban values my family wishes I'd succumb to and my own creativity. My Mum, my sister and my girlfriends all think I should find a rich partner who'll support me. My Dad and my brother think I should abandon the Irish thing and learn to do something lucrative. I'm stubbornly sticking to my rebel path, but I'm suffering because I can't afford to maintain my old car.'

Does Lauren's case sound familiar to you? What can help a creative or unconventional person to rise above the negativity and disapproval of family members? What can help this unique individual to be successful in life, even if she comes from a family that doesn't share her vision or passions?

To help Lauren work through her ambivalent feelings about money, security and where she belongs in her family and in the world, I asked her the following questions. See what your own responses are to these same issues.

- If, miraculously, you were to have the most understanding and supportive family, what specific interests of yours would you want them to understand and support?
- Who might you look to – inside the family and out – for ideas and support on your unconventional path?
- If you were being advised by the best career counsellors and financial advisors in the world, what strategies and steps would you put together as a way of combining your creative passions and your need for a decent cash flow, savings and future financial security?
- Are there any positive traits or useful insights about money or success that you've already learned? Is there

some way that you can become financially secure even if your particular style for making and saving money is quite different from that of your other family members?

Asking Lauren to look beyond her family's particular quirks about money was the beginning of a breakthrough. Like most people, Lauren had limited herself to only two options: either share the family's unappealing money obsessions, or else rebel against your family entirely. A third option that most people forget to consider is, what if you incorporated the best of your family (such as your most financially astute parent's wisdom about money) with other non-family role models as well as your own traits for resilience and creativity?

For several counselling sessions, Lauren and I discussed how much she had learned from watching the financial strengths and weaknesses of a variety of individuals. During one of our conversations, Lauren told me, 'If I could combine my family's financial know-how with my own creative passion for music and culture, that would be a great mixture. My parents and siblings are a little too obsessed with money, but at the same time I do admire their ability to plan for the future and stick with their financial goals. Still, there are creative people I've met over the years who were also persistent and resilient no matter what kinds of difficulties came their way. I suppose there's an aspect of each of these mentors and role models inside me. My job is to make sure I get all these diverse parts of myself working together in harmony.'

Lauren's realization that she could stop competing with her family was the beginning of a process of redefining her own adult identity. She and I started to brainstorm about what specific things she could do to chart her own unique path separately from the sceptical and limited viewpoints of her relatives. Lauren began taking steps to boost her income from several sources that stemmed from her own passion for music and culture. First, she landed a steady job teaching music history as well as a part-time job at a nearby recording studio mixing and arranging songs. Over the next twelve months she also began writing books and articles about some of her favourite folk musicians, and she fulfilled a dream by working as a music producer for a few compilation CDs that did fairly well commercially. Finally, she began saving ten per cent of her income every month towards her future security.

As with many of my creative clients who felt judged or put down by their relatives, Lauren began to build an adult identity that was far beyond what her family could have imagined for her. It allowed her to keep her passions alive by working intelligently at several different ways of making money from her unconventional interests. Two-and-a-half years after she first came in for counselling, Lauren told me, 'I may not be as rich as my brother the doctor, or as comfortable as my money-obsessed sister, but I love where I'm living now and I'm building a future that is both fulfilling and secure. I always thought I'd have to choose between chasing money like my relatives or being poor on my lonely creative path. But now I'm making a good living doing what I care about most in the world. I'm teaching, arranging, writing and producing music. My family still isn't sure what to make of me, but I'm very fortunate. I'm living an authentic life.'

To move beyond comparisons and competition is not easy. But if you take some time to explore the strengths and weaknesses of each of your mentors, role models and most

significant relatives, you will find yourself a little less suscep-
tible to your family's narrow-minded judgments, criticism and
pressure. Most of our family members were too busy dealing
with survival, upward mobility or their fragile egos to have
shown us how to live a healthy and balanced life. The techniques and questions described in this chapter do not aim to
blame your relatives for how they dealt with money or status.
Rather, the purpose of these guidelines is to dig deeply inside
yourself and discover what you want your own life to be
about, to find creative ways to build a life of meaning, purpose and stability. Only then will you have overcome the
pressures of your family.

Do your part to eliminate family favouritism

Now we come to the final step that can change, at least
slightly, the way your family deals with money and status. I
call it the Fairness Coalition. Here's how it works.

- Stop for a moment and think back to a time when a
  member of your family (including yourself) was treated
  badly by relatives who kept him uninformed, or when
  a crucial decision was made without including each of
  the people who should have been included. Or recall a
  time when someone was treated discourteously by your
  relatives because he or she has less education, money or
  status than some of the other family members.

- Recall when someone in your family has given an
  unequal amount of attention, love, financial assistance
  or emotional support to one family member, often at
  the expense of another; for example, when one sibling
  was treated better than another, or, with grandchildren,
  when one set was given more than another.

- Now imagine what might have happened if your favourites-playing relative had been phoned or visited immediately by two or more people and told, 'We don't agree with how this has been done. We need to come up with a fairer solution.' What if any unfairness had been addressed quickly by two or more family members speaking up in a courteous manner?

Most people are uncomfortable with confrontation and reluctant to challenge the status quo in their families. But I have seen repeatedly that if you plan ahead of time, you can set up a calm but powerful Fairness Coalition that can get wonderful things accomplished with a minimum of divisiveness or conflict.

Before the next incident or crisis, spend a few minutes calling or visiting two or more members of your extended family who share your concerns about the unfair treatment that has been going on. Ask these sane and compassionate relatives, 'Are you interested in working as a team to improve how our family deals with issues of money, fairness and equality?' Then brainstorm together about what each of you will do and say the next time there is another example of favouritism by one of your relatives. Decide in advance which of you is the right person to talk to this particular relative calmly and in private to say, 'We need your help on an important matter. We're worried about a situation that is hurting some members of our family. We want to work with you to come up with a solution.'

Please note that this wording is neither disrespectful nor inflammatory. If two or more people talk to a family member who has been guilty of favouritism in this way, it is far more likely that he or she will consider your point of view.

When an incident does occur in the future, you can acti-
vate the Fairness Coalition quickly with just a few phone calls
or e-mails. Within minutes or hours, the family member who
is being unfair will have heard from two or more people who
are asking him or her to do the right thing. If a stubborn or
arrogant family member refuses to budge or insists that he or
she has the right to act unfairly, the Coalition can increase the
pressure. You can bring in a third or a fourth family member,
or a trusted or respected family friend to talk some sense in
to your stubborn relative. In some families it takes several
Fairness Coalition members threatening not to turn up at the
next family event before that relative agrees to be more even-
handed and fair.

I'm not recommending an ugly war of words but rather
a calm, firm conversation that says, 'We are people who care
about you and who care about the family. And we all agree
that for the sake of family harmony you need to be more flexible. We don't want to pull away from you because we care
about you. But if you don't start treating [so-and-so] more
fairly, it's going to be hard for us to be as close to you as we've
been in the past.'

'We need to be unified as a family'

Doreen's case is a good example of how to deal with unequal
treatment and financial favouritism in an extended family.
Doreen is an unmarried woman in her early forties whose
widowed grandmother and financially secure parents helped
her three other siblings with financial support at important
moments in their lives. According to Doreen, 'My older sister, Gwen, got help from my grandmother when she got married and needed a deposit for a new house. My younger
brother, Bruce, got help from both my grandmother and my

parents when he started his own business seven years ago. And my younger sister, Helen, has just had a huge wedding paid for by my parents. I have no idea how much it cost, but the gourmet food and the huge ice sculptures were not what you would call understated.'

So when Doreen saved money from her job as a legal secretary and tried to buy her first flat, she went to her parents and her grandmother to see if they would help her, too, with the deposit. She was disappointed but not surprised when her grandmother said, 'I don't feel happy about giving you money at the moment. Maybe when you finally get married I'll be able to give you a little something.'

Then Doreen spoke to her parents and was told, 'We'll help with the deposit, but we'll need to put our names on the title deeds as owners.'

Doreen asked, 'Why? You didn't feel the need for ownership when you and Grandma helped Gwen buy her first home or when you helped Bruce to start his business. Is it because I'm the only one in the family who's still not married?'

Doreen's parents looked at her impatiently. 'This is just business,' they said. 'We'll help you buy somewhere to live but we need to protect our investment.'

When Doreen told me this, you could see the hurt in her eyes. 'How could they be so insensitive? It's clearly so unfair. I've worked for fourteen years in the same job and been very reliable. Yes, I'm not married with 2.5 kids, but for heaven's sake, I'm in my forties. I'm not a child who's going to fritter away their money. Why do they treat their married children in one way and their unmarried daughter another?'

For the next few counselling sessions we explored the emotional pain that this and other incidents have caused

Doreen. But we also progressed and put together a Fairness Coalition in Doreen's extended family. She called two of her aunts and an uncle, and also had lunch with each of her three siblings.

Like many people who have tried this approach, Doreen found that 'Not everyone agreed with me, and a few people simply didn't have the guts to speak up on my behalf. But I did manage to put together a pretty good Coalition of influential relatives. My uncle, who has always had a great laugh with me at family parties, was quite horrified that my parents were doing this. He and one of my aunts promised me they would take my parents out to dinner in a few days and read them the riot act. My older sister, Gwen, has never been able to stand up to my parents. She said to me, "Look, Doreen, I agree with you in principle. But I think it's wrong to upset Mum and Dad. Can't you just wait until you have a little more of your own money saved up for the deposit?" That's just who Gwen is and I don't know if she'll ever change.'

Doreen added, however, 'I did get a good response from my older brother and my younger sister. They both admitted, "It's not easy going up against Mum and Dad when they become rigid about something. But this is so divisive and unnecessary. We need to be unified as a family and not let our parents split us apart over money. Yes, it's their money and their decision, but it's also important that their children not be divided by resentment or bitterness that could easily be prevented."'

It took a lot of persuasion from the aunt, siblings and uncle before Doreen's parents understood that this was not 'just business'. As Doreen's father explained to her ten days later when he gave her a cheque towards the deposit, 'Please don't think we're bad or that we don't love you, because we think the world of you. But your Mum and I both grew up without a lot of money, and we also grew up at a time when parents simply didn't want to encourage or reward their kids for staying single. Of course we want to help you be happy, and frankly we wish you would find happiness with a husband. But your brother, your sister, your aunts and your uncle each made a strong case that this is not the right time to be pushing you about marriage. They convinced us that this is a pivotal situation when the family is either going to stay unified or else be split apart. And since we don't want a rift in the family, we hope you'll understand that this wasn't easy for us, but we do want to be fair and decent.'

Doreen had tears in her eyes as she thanked her parents. She told me later, 'I could see this was very hard for them. They don't like releasing this much control, especially regarding money. I don't need my Mum and Dad to be perfect. God knows they've got their problems and their imperfections. But I was glad that this forced them to realize that you can't keep treating three of your offspring to generous handouts and the fourth with constant pressure to be different from who she is. I'm glad there were members of the family who were willing to speak up for fairness.'

In your own family, there may be some relatives who choose not to participate in a Fairness Coalition, either because they don't agree with your reasoning or they aren't willing to speak up. That's their right and their decision. But if you reach out to several possible candidates in your extended family as well as outside help from the clergy, financial advisors or family friends whom your difficult relative respects, you will eventually have the makings of a strong coalition of people who care about fairness and who care about you. Then you will have the tools to improve the level of mutual respect and equal treatment in your family. Good luck!

CHAPTER SEVEN

HOW TO DEAL WITH DRUGS, ALCOHOL AND OTHER ADDICTIONS

When I was twelve years old I saw on late-night television a black-and-white version of the classic film *Dr Jekyll and Mr Hyde*, based on the famous story by Robert Louis Stevenson in which a dignified and articulate gentleman unleashes his uninhibited, aggressive, guilt-free alter ego each time he sips a powerful cocktail of mood-altering chemicals. One minute the well-educated Dr Jekyll appears to be kind and considerate; the next, after he ingests the mysterious potion, his personality changes dramatically, revealing the selfish and uncaring Mr Hyde.

That film has always stayed with me as a metaphor for what happens when a family member has a problem with alcohol, drugs, gambling or some other addiction. One minute this beloved relative can be delightful and charming, but when he or she has had 'one too many', a very different and unpleasant subpersonality emerges, and the rest of the family is stuck having to deal with this person's boorish behaviour.

There are tens of thousands of other men and women who become hostile, domineering or aggressive when they have more to drink than they should. Since most of these problem drinkers have at least a few family members who find themselves on the receiving end of this person's alcohol-related unpleasantness, we're talking about a lot of uncomfortable moments.

According to government statistics, there are also a large number of us who have to deal with a family member who has a drug problem. As well as the people who use illegal drugs, there are thousands of adults who experience serious side-effects from the overuse of painkillers, sedatives and other prescription drugs.

If someone in your family has a problem with alcohol, drugs, gambling or another addiction, you may have experienced one or more of the following situations.

- Pretending your relative isn't acting strangely when you know that he is at it again.
- Feeling like a gullible fool each time this person persuades you to believe that she will be more considerate but then begins behaving unpleasantly again.
- Playing detective, trying to work out the lies and evasive comments that this person has told you in order to mislead you about his problem.
- Wondering if the situation would be better if only you knew the right thing to do or say.
- Getting caught into helping your relative hide the problem from others in the family, or from neighbours, bosses, friends or colleagues.
- Asking your family member before a family party, 'Could you please not overdo it this time?' and getting an angry response that says or implies, 'Mind your own business'.
- Repeatedly asking this person to seek help so that his addiction doesn't continue to increase family tension.

• Screaming at this person that you can't continue to live like this, yet finding yourself unable to keep to your threats or to get much of a distance from the twists and turns of this person's life.

FACING THE TRUTH ABOUT ADDICTION

If a relative's dependence on alcohol, drugs, gambling or other addictions were easy to change, I wouldn't need to write this chapter and you wouldn't need to read it. But if you listen to the accounts of men and women who have got a little too close to addictive habits, you will see how hard it is to break free once you are hooked. Here are a few examples of things I've heard. See if any of these stories sound familiar to you.

> I have one client who continues to insist that he is not a problem drinker, even though his wife and children have told me on several occasions that whenever he's had two or more glasses of wine, they notice that the caring and considerate father and husband they love tends to disappear for a couple of hours, replaced by an angry, impatient, controlling – well, Mr Hyde. 'He'll often say or do something that makes our dinner guests wonder why we put up with his ugly behaviour. But if we mention it to him, he'll laugh and say, "You are exaggerating. I barely had any wine. It takes a lot more than that before I've had too much."'

> Recently I counselled a man who told me, 'I used to do a few hits of marijuana only on special occasions – to celebrate some success or to pick me up

when I'm having an especially hard day. But now I crave a few joints even when there's nothing much to celebrate and no crisis to resolve. I just like the familiar feeling of the paper between my fingers, lighting up and drawing in that bittersweet smoky escape from my life. Recently I've made any excuse to sneak out behind the garage and have a few puffs. It's heaven and I don't really care if my wife doesn't approve.'

A few years ago I counselled a woman who had lost two jobs, suffered the break-up of a great relationship, filed for bankruptcy and alienated her two adult children because of her recurring addiction to gambling. Yet this intelligent woman looked me right in the eyes and said, 'I have my gambling under control; I always know when to get out. I just do it because it's fun. The sounds and the smells inside the casino are deliciously tacky. When I'm picking the right numbers and the winnings are piling up in front of me, time stops and I'm completely at peace for a few moments. What's so bad about being at peace, surrounded by a crowd of new acquaintances all having fun and feeling alive?'

Many years ago I counselled a woman who was very successful at her high-pressure job, and quite charming to talk to, but she admitted during one of our sessions, 'I'm outwardly strong but terrified inside most of the time. The one relief I get is when I pour myself a good stiff martini. Watching the liquid swirl around, hearing the clink of the ice cube against the glass and then bringing it up to my lips – the whole ritual is like being with an exquisite lover who makes me feel relaxed, secure and completely protected. I have had a love affair with these delicious martinis ever since the first time they helped me blot out my insecure feelings. My business colleagues and my boyfriend have begged me to stop because they say it makes me hazy and forgetful, but no one in my life realizes just how much I need this daily dose of relief that always takes the edge off no matter how much pressure I'm under.'

The light bulb has to really want to change

When I hear stories like the four listed above from people who are strongly attracted to alcohol, drugs or gambling – and believe me, I hear many – I often think of the old light bulb joke concerning psychotherapy. It goes like this.

Question: How many therapists does it take to change a light bulb?

Answer: The light bulb has to really want to change.

It doesn't matter how much you want your family member to recover, improve, change or grow. What matters is the motivation and persistence of your troubled relative. His desire for change is the ingredient that determines whether or not he is going to get better.

The good news is that some of our family members *are* motivated to change; they just need some help from non-judgmental but honest family members to make sure they stay on track. The bad news is that most *aren't* sufficiently motivated, and no amount of badgering, coaxing, confronting or manipulating is going to help.

Can our own loved ones break free of their compulsions? Can we ever be free of the difficult behaviour caused by their dependency? Can therapy or rehabilitation programmes help? Can books, tapes or medication make a difference? To determine all this, think about your relative's true degree of motivation. Would you say this family member was extremely motivated to change this habit? Or would you say this person is slightly motivated but easily thrown off track? Or would you have to admit that your family member is seriously resistant or reluctant to change, despite how much the rest of you have been trying to convince this person of the need for change?

This kind of honesty is important because if you keep pretending your family member is more motivated than he or she truly is, then you are also living in a state of denial. Breaking out of denial and admitting the truth about your family member is the first step towards reclaiming your own sanity and freedom.

STRATEGIES FOR DEALING WITH AN ADDICTED FAMILY MEMBER

If you want to save yourself and your non-addicted family members a lot of wasted effort and ugly power struggles, here are three things you can do to be more effective in responding to a troubled or addicted family member. None of these strategies is guaranteed or invincible, but I have seen them lead to significant improvements in the majority of families who tried them. If you want to create a little more serenity and a lot less frustration in your family, consider doing one or more of the following.

Discuss how this person's behaviour is affecting the family

In most families there is a lot of tiptoeing around alcohol, drug, gambling or other addiction problems. To break out of this dishonesty, invite each member of the family to a brain-storming session to consider the following questions:

- What are your worries about bringing outsiders to family events in light of your family member's unpleasant behaviour?
- When have you felt personally attacked, ignored, mistreated or let down by the family member who has been engaging in addictive habits?
- What have you been saying to yourself to excuse this person or to deny that it's affecting your life?
- What have you begun to do to compensate or cover for this person?
- What do you imagine your family interactions could be like if this person were to get help and change his or her unpleasant behaviour?
- In what ways has this person's difficult behaviour caused you to become less trusting or more cut off from other people in your life?
- Has the chaos generated by this troubled person caused you to be sidetracked or too distracted to give your best to some creative project or important relationship?

These concerns are to be written down and then spoken aloud without attacking the addicted person's character or underlying goodness. We're talking here about problem behaviour and not about someone's soul or worth as a person. But we do need to get each family member's reactions out on the table so we can assess the full impact of the addicted person's behaviour.

In some families, where the troubled individual is a caring and non-defensive person, this fact-finding discussion about the impact on the family can take place with the addicted person present. In other cases, where the addicted person is too fragile, too defensive or too volatile to be included in the initial discussion, the family should first meet without him or her there.

In either case, the goal of this meeting is not to criticize the troubled individual who has an addiction problem, but rather to assess how the addiction is influencing each of the other family members. For while the family is locked in silence or denial regarding the elephant in the room that no one is allowed to mention, healing and change will be blocked.

'She had no idea how we all felt'

Edward's situation is a good example of what can happen when there's a family meeting to bring together everyone's different insights and reactions about an addicted family member. Edward came to one of my workshops on dealing with difficult family members. Afterwards he told me that he is a 56-year-old accountant whose 59-year-old sister, Sheila, is a divorced nurse with two grown-up children. Sheila suffered a serious back injury several years ago and started taking prescription medication to help her sleep and to reduce pain.

According to Edward, 'Sheila became a little too fond of her medication and it got to the point where she was becoming addicted. She started to lose her memory, she became extremely moody at times, and she was acting oddly because of the side-effects. My other two siblings and I were quite worried about her. We'd heard rumours that she was starting to act unprofessionally at work, and she'd broken up with her most recent boyfriend, who told us he was tired of living with her constant mood swings since she'd been taking so many pills.'

In phone calls and at family gatherings, Edward and his siblings tried to reason with Sheila that she had become addicted and needed help. But Sheila laughed at their suggestion, saying, 'You don't know anything. I've got this under control. After all, I'm a nurse and you don't have any experience except the nonsense you read on the internet.'

Then a few months later Sheila nearly died in a car crash because she fell asleep at the wheel. Edward thought the car accident would have an impact on Sheila. But like many people who have a fondness for a particular addictive substance, Sheila came out of hospital with an even stronger desire to keep herself medicated with higher doses of painkillers than her doctor had prescribed. Using her connections as a nurse, Sheila managed to coax a few doctors to prescribe supplies of her favourite pills.

A few weeks after Sheila was released from the hospital, Edward called each of his siblings and they decided to organize a family meeting the next Sunday that would include Sheila, all her siblings, Sheila's two adult children and Sheila's work friend Josie, a nurse who had battled a similar type of addiction to pain medication several years earlier. When Edward first asked Sheila to come, she was hesitant, saying, 'You're wasting your time. I've got this under control.' But when Edward said to her, 'Listen, Sheila, you're a nurse. You should be there on Sunday. You can explain to us exactly what you're taking and why we should stop worrying. And you can listen while we each tell you what it's been like for us these past few months watching someone we love in so much distress. I think we all need to have this kind of an open and honest conversation. What do you say?' Sheila paused for a moment and then said, 'Fine. I'll be there. Someone's got to make sure you get the facts straight.'

Before the meeting, Edward did two things that I recommended to him to help make the family discussion more successful. First, he reminded each of the family members and friends that they should be honest about their concerns but not attack Sheila or criticize her. Research has shown that compassionately telling your troubled family member how much you care about him or her and how frustrating it is to have your life turned upside down by their refusal to seek help is usually enough to spur them into seeking help.

Second, Edward reminded Sheila several times during the days leading up to the family meeting that 'Each of us loves you, Sheila, and we always will. We all know you are a good Mum, a great sister, an excellent nurse and a good friend. This meeting is to work out if the side-effects of the medication are changing your behaviour in ways that would happen to any of us if we were in the same painful situation you've been in. It's not about judging you. It's about hearing your ideas on what the medication is or isn't doing, and about what each of us has experienced over the past few months. It's a chance for all of us to share information without attacking or criticizing one another.' This type of clarification of the purpose of a family meeting is crucial. It lets your troubled loved one know that he or she is still a respected and worthwhile human being, even if his or her addictive behaviour has been getting on people's nerves.

The family meeting on Sunday afternoon started out rather awkwardly when Sheila announced, 'I just want you guys to know I appreciate your concern but I'm fine and I don't need any help.' As Edward told me a few days later, 'I believed at that moment this was going to be a fiasco. My know-it-all sister Sheila was not going to listen.'

Yet after each of the gathered relatives and friends had spoken honestly and lovingly about how much things had changed as a result of the medication problems, Sheila's eyes filled with tears. She told them, 'This is very hard to listen to. I never thought my little problem was causing so much discomfort to those who mean so much to me.'

Edward told me several weeks later, 'That meeting was the first of several key moments in Sheila's recovery. She had no idea how we all felt until we sat down and finally got her to take us seriously. That meeting led to Sheila joining a twelve-step programme that specializes in prescription drug addictions. She began going to meetings, talking at least once a day with her sponsor, and reading the recovery stories of men and women whose behaviour, moods and memory had been temporarily affected by pain medications and sleeping pills. It's been hard work, but Sheila's made a lot of progress getting the drugs out of her system and repairing the damage they did to her work, her personal life and her family relationships.'

Don't get into a power struggle

Not everyone has the kind of satisfying breakthrough that occurred for Edward and his sister Sheila. Sometimes the caring family members are less able to bring about positive change. As I mentioned earlier, sometimes the addicted family member is too fragile, too defensive or too volatile to attend a family meeting. So you need to know about the other options that might help and, above all, how to avoid making things worse.

'I could kill the bastard'

Gerard is a 34-year-old film editor whose father-in-law, John, a successful businessman in his sixties, came to my office to seek help. According to John, 'My son-in-law Gerard is in trouble and he just refuses to deal with it. We knew when my daughter Julianne met Gerard six years ago that he was a bit of a drinker, but we had no idea the problems this would cause. In the past few months Gerard has been drinking a lot more than we'd realized. A few weeks ago he lost an important customer after getting tipsy and way too talkative at an important industry fund-raiser. Then Gerard smashed up his new car by driving home drunk and plowing it through the interior wall of the garage. Last week my daughter finally told us that Gerard's been having several glasses of wine each night before dinner and screaming at their two young toddlers whenever the kids misbehave in even the most normal ways. Frankly, I'm worried about my daughter and I'm worried about our grandchildren.'

A week before John called me, he had tried on his own to set up a family intervention to confront Gerard about his drinking problem. It backfired. John's daughter Julianne got upset during a phone call a few days before the scheduled intervention and accused her parents of trying to undermine her marriage. Gerard heard about the proposed intervention and told his wife that she was to stop calling or visiting her parents until they apologized to him personally. John's wife, Gladys, was thinking about calling social services to come and investigate whether the two young children were safe living with an explosive drinker; John and his wife were debating day and night about whether or not to call for help. As you often find in families where there is an addicted individual, everyone was feeling agitated and upset.

During our initial conversation I tried to support John's frustration at feeling powerless to help his daughter get her husband into treatment. Like most family members of an addicted person, he was feeling a justified fear that his daughter and her kids were heading for a long bout of chaos and unpleasantness.

But I also noticed that he had only harsh things to say about his son-in-law, and he seemed determined to use the recent drinking incidents as a justification for telling Julianne her marriage was over. John told me, 'I am not going to let my only daughter ruin her life by staying married to this bastard. She deserves so much better than this.'

I told him his feelings were understandable. It's very painful to be a parent and watch your grown-up children make decisions you disagree with. But I also asked him, 'Do you know why your daughter married Gerard? Is there a good side to him that she's still in love with?'

John answered quickly, 'I haven't the slightest clue.'

Then I asked him, 'Would you be willing to talk to her calmly and hear her side of the story?'

He snapped back, 'What would be the point? The guy is a complete loser. Sure he makes a decent salary, but it's just a matter of time before he ruins that, too.'

My goal at this point in the counselling session was to help John see that he was reducing his chances of being effective by remaining so stubborn and controlling. It's a normal human reaction to want to jump in and mend or give orders to a troubled family member. But it usually tends to make things worse. I said to John in a calm voice, 'Do you realize that you don't sound at all interested in your daughter's side of the story? I know you love her, but would you be willing to hear the reasons why she married Gerard and why she's hoping to stay in the marriage?'

John looked at me with a sour expression on his face, and I doubted he was feeling too thrilled at this moment that he had come in for counselling. I looked at him and said, 'I imagine that you are a person who doesn't like being told what to do.'

'Too right,' he replied.

'Well, neither does your daughter and neither does your son-in-law. If you want to be effective with them, you need to start listening and stop giving orders.'

John commented, 'That won't be easy, especially since I could kill the bastard.'

I smiled and said, 'No, it's not going to be easy. But do you think you can start listening and stop giving orders?'

John puffed out his chest and said, 'I can do anything if I try hard enough.'

That was the beginning of a breakthrough for John and his family. Like many intelligent and successful people, John had felt furious that an addiction was creating such havoc in his life. Yet as they teach in Al-Anon and other programmes for helping family members cope with an addicted or troubled family member, 'The sooner you stop trying to rush in and control everything and everyone, the sooner things can begin to change.'

The next week, John and his daughter Julianne met for lunch. John began by apologizing and said, 'I've been seeing a counsellor to talk about what's been going on in our family. I've been told that I've been somewhat bossy and rude towards you and your marriage. The counsellor said I've never really stopped to consider your feelings about why you fell in love with Gerard and why you're working so hard to keep the marriage going. Is that true?'

Julianne grinned and took her father's hand, 'Oh, Dad, you're something else. I never thought I'd see the day when you'd apologize for being bossy or you'd ask to hear my feelings about something you'd already made up your mind about.'

Then she went on to describe what a passionate, intelligent and kind-hearted person Gerard can be when he's not drinking, and what a great father he is when he's sober. She had tears in her eyes as she said, 'I still love my husband but I'm worried about him. Gerard's Mum had a drinking problem and she was also diagnosed as manic-depressive or bipolar. I'm hoping Gerard will get help, but there are two obstacles we've got to overcome. First of all, Gerard won't go to Alcoholics Anonymous because he loathes the "higher power" language they use. I love the support I've had from Al-Anon over the past few months. But Gerard flips when they talk about turning things over to God.'

Julianne continued, 'The second obstacle is that Gerard won't stop drinking for long enough to see if any of the bipolar medications help. We've been told by our specialist that many people are like Gerard – using an ineffective drug such as alcohol to self-medicate a serious illness like depression. But the effective anti-depressants don't work very well if there's alcohol messing up your biochemistry. I think Gerard understands the problem but he's having trouble accepting that his drinking is an inefficient way of dealing with an underlying biochemical problem that needs serious treatment.'

As John told me a few days later, 'I was stunned sitting there and looking at my grown-up daughter, whom I thought I had to protect all this time. She'd been dealing with her husband's problems quite intelligently. She was miles ahead of me on this one.'

I congratulated John for realizing that he was going to need to treat his daughter with respect and to find a way to be of service to her without undermining her strength. Then I asked him an even tougher question: 'Would you be willing to attend a counselling session in which Gerard is invited to tell his side of the story to you and your wife? My experience has been that addicts and troubled family members don't like to be lectured, but they do turn up and sometimes they even become more cooperative if the family promises to listen to them talking about their own struggle.'

John glared at me but then he took a deep breath and said, 'If that's what it takes.'

'I don't want to keep spoiling things'

A week later Gerard walked into my office on the understanding that the other family members were required to listen while he explained his own point of view about his difficulties with mood swings and drinking. As I've found with many addicted individuals, Gerard was a lot more pleasant to be with when he sensed that he was going to be listened to rather than when he thought he was going to be outnumbered or criticized.

At this family session I asked Gerard a version of the non-threatening and usually successful question that was discussed earlier in Chapters Two and Three: 'Would you be willing to tell your in-laws what you believe works and what doesn't work to make things healthier and less contentious in your family?'

For a few minutes, Gerard began to complain about all the times John and Gladys had been condescending or controlling towards him and Julianne. He was expecting John to disagree or cut him off, but instead John just listened. After a few minutes,

Gerard relaxed a bit and then he turned to Julianne and said, 'I don't want to keep spoiling things and making life hard for you and the children. I know I've got a problem, but I absolutely will not go into some programme where they want me to believe in something spiritual or religious. That's just not who I am.'

At that moment I sensed that Gerard was as open to change as he was ever going to be. Even though I happen to love the twelve-step programmes that help men and women focus on their higher power (in whatever way they imagine that higher power to exist), I recognize that for lots of people the spiritual terminology is off-putting. So I suggested to Gerard, 'Would you be willing to investigate recovery programmes that don't insist on phrases you don't feel comfortable using? There are a few that have helped people like yourself. One uses acupuncture and holistic remedies to help people stop drinking. Another uses non-religious approaches to help people manage their cravings and addictions.'

Gerard looked at me with a bit of hesitation and an equal measure of interest. He took a deep breath and said, 'I'll check out one or two and see what they're like.'

I complimented Gerard on his courage. 'It takes guts to tackle these issues. I'm sure there are going to be some difficult moments as part of your recovery. But this is one of the most important things you've ever done for yourself, your wife and your children.'

Gerard smiled. It was the first time I'd seen his face light up in a smile.

We could have stopped there, but I didn't want to focus just on the drinking. Quite often our troubled family members need help with more than one thing if they are gong to be successful in their recovery. So I asked Gerard and Julianne if they'd be willing during the next few months to start an anger-management course designed for parents of young children, and also to consult a psychiatrist who is an expert on medication for bipolar disorders. They agreed to give it a try.

I can't promise that even half of the problem drinkers and drug users in our families will be as willing as Gerard was to try a healthier alternative. Experience has shown me that almost half of all people with addictions are simply unwilling or unable to follow through on positive changes. But what worked for John, Gladys, Julianne and Gerard is the same basic principle that has worked for many others. We need to stop trying to control or demonize the addicted person and explore creative options for those who haven't yet been successful in their recoveries. Today, there are numerous twelve-step programmes and alternative therapies that are quite effective. Without getting into a power struggle, simply give your troubled family member the information and encouragement he needs to make his own choice.

The other important lesson from this case is that a substantial percentage of people who are drawn to alcohol, drugs, gambling, and other habits are essentially trying to self-medicate and get relief from their underlying depression, anxiety, mood swings, shyness, physical discomfort or emotional insecurity. Rather than judging or condemning this wounded individual, it might be more effective to understand that he or she didn't set out to become an addict. In most cases the drinking, drugs or gambling is just a form of relief or escape that went too far and took on a biochemical urgency that is hard to resist. Seeing this person's addiction as a hard-to-change biochemical problem takes some of the stigma out of the addiction. It can allow your family member to save face while seeking treatment for a 'chemical imbalance' rather than for a character weakness.

Don't overreact to each incident

A third and final issue of concern for the caring family members of people with addictions is how to deal with each setback, or slip. Each time your troubled relative makes some progress you will be tempted to think or feel, 'The worst is over. We're on our way to success.' And each time your troubled relative has a setback, you will be tempted to think or feel, 'Here we go again. There's no hope.'

Rather than bouncing between these two extremes, it helps to see the recovery process in more accurate terms as a complicated mixture of daily steps forwards and occasional steps backwards. Even the strongest and most highly motivated individuals will still have cravings, urges and possibly relapses or slips. Your job is not to be shocked, horrified or pessimistic when these setbacks occur.

'Every few months there's another desperate phone call'
Gillian is a 31-year-old mother of two young children who has spent much of her life trying to help her troubled mother, Kristina, an attractive and charming woman in her fifties who lights up the room wherever she goes. As Gillian described her, 'My mother has always been able to get excellent jobs and attract some exciting boyfriends. But her recurring episodes with alcohol, drugs and gambling have caused her to get fired from several jobs, and each relationship ends up in fights, angry separations, desperate attempts at reconciliation and eventual messy break-ups. I feel sorry for my Mum because she's so dynamic and yet so fragile.'

Gillian came for counselling a few years ago because, in her own words, 'The constant drama from my mama is wearing me down. I try to put some distance between us but she's still my mother and when she calls in some sort of crisis or heartbreak I feel back in the same old trap, trying to mother a stubborn woman who has never grown up. I try to focus on my own work, my own two children, and my husband. But every few months there's another desperate phone call where Mum needs emergency cash or a lift to casualty because she's been beaten up by one of her boyfriends. Every time the phone rings, I get this huge adrenalin surge and worry that it's yet another crisis.'

Gillian continued, 'Mum has taken part in several treatment programmes and she always convinces the staff that she's sincere and motivated. But a few weeks later we invariably get a phone call and it's my dear old Mum, in trouble again. If I let her, she is going to get us into serious financial trouble through having to pay off her gambling and other debts. Plus all the times we turn our lives upside down to come and rescue her from some messy disaster. It's starting to affect my job, my marriage and my sanity.'

Like many of us who have addicted family members that slip and relapse every so often, Gillian needed help in three areas: what to do when her mother calls with another 'emergency'; when to say 'Yes, I'll help up to a limit'; and how to say with less guilt, 'No, Mum, you've got to do that for yourself or with someone else's help besides mine.'

These are tough choices, and I don't think there are simple answers that apply to all situations. But I'll describe what Gillian and I developed as her 'keep the sanity' approach to her difficult Mum. Then you can decide for yourself (or with the help of your own advisers) what strategies to use when your family member relapses or has a dramatic crisis that pulls you in.

The goal is to combine compassion with realistic limits. Some people err too far on the side of unlimited compassion and their addicted relatives often treat them like pushovers. On the other hand, some people lean too far towards cold limit setting or anger and miss out on the chance to help a troubled family member who could benefit from a warmer approach. In between the two extremes is a large middle zone of compassionate limit setting. It's not always easy to work out what your limits are or how to set them in a compassionate way. But if you master this essential skill, you will not only learn how to deal more effectively with an addicted relative but with every other manipulative individual in your life, including volatile teenage children, dishonest ex-spouses, pushy neighbours and two-faced colleagues at work.

Here are the three steps that Gillian tried out for staying sane in spite of what she liked to call her 'drama mama':

Step 1: Decide ahead of time what you're willing to do and what is too much. Gillian and her husband, Lawrence, sat down and decided in advance what they would do next time Gillian's mother called with a financial crisis or other emergency. They weighed several possibilities of what they believed a good son-in-law and daughter should do. They eventually decided that based on their own financial situation and their other family responsibilities, they would set aside a limited budget of £500 (around $1,300 AUD or $1,400 NZD) per year for helping Kristina if she got in a crisis, and be willing to make a maximum of one long drive, train journey of flight each year to help Kristina if she got into a jam and needed immediate assistance.

As Gillian explained it, 'Lawrence and I didn't want to be cruel or cold, but neither did we want my mother's chaotic life to put us in debt or stop us from being able to do all we wanted for our own children. So we decided on how much help we could offer and we wrote my mother a courteous

and considerate letter telling her that while we love her enormously, we don't have unlimited money or time to help her
when she's in crisis. We said how sorry we were to have to
admit we are only human, but we do need to set a yearly
maximum for the foreseeable future.'

A few days after she sent the letter, Gillian called me to
say, 'My Mum got the letter and she's really pissed off. But
you warned us she would be angry. And I think we were quite
decent and loving in the way we told her what we could do
to help and what would be too much to expect.'

As often happens when we set compassionate limits
with an addicted relative, Kristina gave Gillian the silent treatment for several days. I assured Gillian, however, 'There's a
98 per cent chance that she'll call as soon as she misses you
or needs you.' Sure enough, ten days later Gillian and
Lawrence got a desperate phone call from Kristina asking for
help with her laptop computer, which Lawrence is good at
fixing. As Gillian told me, 'Mum never even mentioned our
earlier disagreement about the limits we were setting. She just
acted as if nothing had happened. We were right back to business as usual, except that now we had warned her that we are
human and we do have limits.'

**Step 2: Become a loving brick wall during tough
times.** Whether intentionally or simply by virtue of being a
distressed addict, your family member will almost certainly
test your limits – over and over again. What I urge counselling
clients to do is to practise ahead of time saying silently to
yourself a few magic words that can help you stay focused
and strong during a difficult moment with your addicted family member. These magic words are, 'Loving brick wall. Loving brick wall.' By saying these few words to yourself at least
twice, you prepare your mind to be firm but compassionate

with anyone who is trying to push you past your limits. Then when your distressed family member tries to use a guilt trip to get you to ignore the limits you've set, you will have a powerful antidote that can keep you centred and compassionate.

At the precise moment you are on the phone or talking in person with this troubled family member who is trying to get you to do something unreasonable to help him or her during a crisis, you can say to yourself silently, 'Loving brick wall. Loving brick wall.' Instead of yelling angrily at your relative or acting like a passive victim, just saying those words can help you stay focused as you restate your limits.

For example, the first 'loving brick wall' test for Gillian came eight weeks after she sent her mother the letter spelling out the limits that would apply during a crisis. Her mother phoned from Monte Carlo to say that she had been arrested for writing dodgy cheques on her employer's bank account to cover her gambling debts. Upset and talking rapidly, Kristina wanted Gillian and her husband to fly immediately to Monte Carlo to bail her out for £5000 (around $13,000 AUD or $14,000 NZD) and also to help fund a lawyer to 'beat these ridiculous charges'.

Normally Gillian would have dropped everything to rush in and try to help her troubled parent. But this time Gillian took a deep breath and silently said to herself the words we had practised, 'Loving brick wall. Loving brick wall.' Then she said audibly and calmly into the phone, 'Mum, I love you and I'm sorry you're in a horrible spot. I wish we could do more to help. But as I said eight weeks ago, the most we can come up with is £500 per year for emergency expenses like a lawyer. We also can't risk jeopardizing our jobs and our children by rushing over to Monaco.

I can make one emergency trip a year, but not more than that. Do you think this should be the time for me to cancel work, get a babysitter and come to you? I'll do it if it's absolutely necessary. Or do you want me to save up my one stint off work in case you need it later on?'

'You can shove it up your ass,' was Kristina's reply. 'I don't want you here if that's your attitude.'

Gillian said silently, 'Loving brick wall. Loving brick wall.' Then she said audibly and warmly into the phone, 'Listen, Mum. I love you and I care about you a lot. But you're going to have to live with the consequences of writing illegal cheques on your boss's bank account. I didn't do that and Lawrence didn't do that. You did that. I'm going to be on your side no matter what, but if you need more than £500 it will have to come from some other friends or relatives this time. I'm so sorry. I wish I could do more, but you and I have already talked about this. Lawrence and I are human and we have to set some healthy limits.'

Kristina was crying as she said, 'Why are you doing this to me? I'm your mother....'

Gillian took a deep breath and slowed down her racing pulse by repeating silently the words, 'Loving brick wall. Loving brick wall.' Then she said to her mother, 'I'm doing this because I care about you. I've got two children, a husband, a job and financial commitments. I wish I could do more to help, but I truly believe that you'll find a way to learn and grow from this. I just hope we can stay close no matter what because I love you and you'll always be my Mum.'

Kristina swore and hung up the phone at that point. But she called the next day to say, 'I'm sorry. I was a bit hungover last night. I know you love me and I didn't mean some of the things I said to you.'

As I've found with many clients who have had to set limits with their addicted relatives, it's never easy. But the challenge is to be realistic about what you can offer and what will push you over the edge into resentment or financial trouble. Even if your relative puts up a fuss, it's far more decent to be honest and compassionate, to be a 'loving brick wall', than to let someone push you past your limits, which will usually destroy the relationship with feelings of bitterness and victimization. The best way to keep loving a troubled or addicted person is to remind her that you exist and that you are going to take care of yourself so that you don't burn out or get destroyed by the chaos.

Step 3: Get support so you can be a consistent and strong ally (but never a doormat) for your troubled relative. With each relapse, emergency or crisis you will be tested. If you do your best to breathe, stay calm and accept that your compassionate limits are not cruel, you will probably be able to weather the storms and keep your sanity. You may need the wisdom, experience and fellowship of others in an Al-Anon or some other carers' support programme. You may need to phone supportive friends each time you begin wondering, 'Is it wrong to say no to someone who's making unreasonable demands? Is it cruel to tell an addicted family member that we're all human and we have limits, too?'

In Gillian's case, getting support from Al-Anon was especially important because Kristina kept trying to blame Gillian and her husband for her own legal difficulties. For several days after her arrest, Kristina kept calling and insisting she wanted them to come to Monaco with a large sum of money to bail her out. Gillian stayed strong, however, and told her mother, 'I'll help you find a good lawyer and I'll pay the first £500 of legal fees. But the rest of the money is going to have to come from your other friends and relatives.' Kristina ended up borrowing most of the legal costs from one of her ex-boyfriends, and she put up a good defence before being sentenced to six months in prison and a fine for forging the cheques.

Despite how painful it was knowing how unhappy her mother was in jail, Gillian found that, 'After the first few weeks in prison my Mum seemed to grow up a bit from the double whammy of my setting limits on her and also from being in a place where they didn't care how good looking or charming she was. I think the boring prison clothes, the bad food and the fact that my husband and I continued to give her emotional support with weekly phone calls and several visits made her realize that we do love her. One afternoon I was sitting with her in the visiting area and she said to me, "Gillian, you're tough sometimes, but I'm glad you're strong. Because if you weren't strong, I would probably have worn you out by now."'

Gillian said of her Mum, 'I think she was somewhat humbled from being in jail and that's helped her become serious about working towards recovery. So far, during the first twelve months since she's been out of prison, she's stayed sober, stopped gambling and worked hard at her new job. I can't predict the future, but I'm glad we got out of the business of doing too much for Mum and then resenting her for it. This whole ordeal has taught me a lot about patience, firmness and being able to set limits lovingly, which I'm probably going to need with my children when they're teenagers. And I've finally found a way to just love my Mum and not carry the full burden of trying to rescue her. Only Kristina can rescue Kristina, with the love and support of all of us who have stuck by her. Most importantly, I think I'm finally starting to learn that she's supposed to be the Mum and I'm supposed to be the daughter. It took a long time to work out that my job is not to take away her problems. My job is to let her know that I care about her and that I'm only human.'

If you, too, have a family member who sometimes brings chaos to your life or who frequently tests your limits, my hope is that this stressful relationship will sooner or later bring you crucial insights like it did for Gillian and many others I have counselled. Our most troubled relatives often indirectly make us learn about patience, persistence, limit setting and compassion. I wish there were an easier way to learn these important things, but for now all we can do is appreciate that our addicted relatives might be helping us grow much more than we ever thought possible.

CHAPTER EIGHT

IS THERE ANYTHING YOU CAN DO ABOUT INTOLERANT RELATIVES?

Have you ever witnessed any overt or subtle racism in your family? For example, is there someone in your family who tends to say condescending or contemptuous things about people of other races? Or possibly someone in your family who has what is called 'internalized racism' and can't stop criticizing or seeing only the worst traits in your own race or ethnic group?

Have you detected any severe or mild sexism in your family? Is there someone in your family who says hostile things towards women who aren't passive and sweet all the time? Does he try to feel big by making cruel jokes or insensitive comments at family gatherings? Is there someone who gives first-class treatment and lots of encouragement to one gender, but gives second-class treatment and harsh criticism to the other?

Have you noticed any homophobic remarks or insulting comments about sexual orientation in your family? Do you have a relative who has rigid ideas about what is right for a boy and what is right for a girl for fear that someone might be 'different?' Or a family member who would be uncomfortable if you introduced her to someone who is gay, lesbian,

bisexual or transgendered? (A transgendered person is someone who feels more at home in the clothes, behaviour, or
actual body of the other gender.) Have you ever got into a
frustrating argument with a family member about homosexuality and felt as if the conversation went nowhere?

If you answered yes to any of the above questions, you
are not alone. Over the years I've found that nearly every
family has at least one of these kinds of conflicts. Even if no
single relative flaunts the fact that he's racist, sexist or homophobic, I'm willing to bet there might still be some of these
feelings just under the surface. Quite often people think
they've moved beyond the prejudices and intolerance of past
generations, but then a family member announces that he's in
love with someone very different from what the family had
been expecting. At those moments, powerful feelings may
flare up unexpectedly, and sometimes we hear loved ones say
things we never thought we'd hear.

This chapter will explore a controversial topic that I
have rarely seen addressed in books on personal growth or
family relations – not so much the politics of racism, sexism
and homophobia, but more the personal side of these issues.
I'd also like to introduce you to approaches that can help you
deal with hurtful comments that you witness – or are the tar-
get of – in your own family.

HOW TO RESPOND TO
A PREJUDICED RELATIVE

If someone in your family says or does something that offends
you (or is intolerant or hurtful toward someone you care
about), should you simply ignore it? Should you just shrug it
off and say, 'My relative is insensitive and small-minded.

There's nothing I can do about it.' Or would you like to be able to respond in an effective way?

For more than 20 years I have been a consultant and adviser for several organizations on the family aspects and psychological roots of intolerance. My focus has been on how to respond when someone in your family causes you pain because he or she is hostile or mistrustful towards a certain group of people. I have found that if you want to make an impact on your intolerant relative, there are three specific approaches that dramatically improve your chances.

Clarify your own reasons for caring about the issue

Quite often people who feel hurt by an offensive remark become self-righteous and immediately start name-calling or judging the relative who made the remark. 'You're such a racist', or 'You sexist pig', or 'You are seriously homophobic' might be your or another family member's response. Within seconds, the conversation turns into a row or the person is ignoring you. Instead of making an impact on your hurtful relative, that person puts up an emotional wall and thinks to himself, 'I'm right and this ridiculous bleeding-heart, politically correct twit in front of me is wrong.'

That's why I recommend trying something less political and more personal. The most powerful thing you can do in response to a hurtful remark is to stop, take a breath, and then clarify in a heart-to-heart way why you are so hurt or upset by what was just said or done. It requires being honest and vulnerable, which might not be your first reaction to an intolerant or bigoted relative. But if you take a moment to investigate your own feelings about this issue, you will find it often leads to much greater success.

'I've never been honest with you about this'

For example, one of my clients is Robert, a 28-year-old teacher who grew up in an upwardly mobile family where his hardworking parents thought they were being fair to each of their three children. But in fact, according to Robert, as the darkest-skinned member of the family he tended to receive less affection, less attention and less encouragement than his two lighter-skinned siblings. 'I know my parents and grand-parents loved me,' said Robert, 'but they had much higher hopes and confidence in my brother and sister who could mingle more easily in affluent circles. And when my Dad's father died, he left a somewhat larger sum to both of my siblings, as if to say to me, "You're a risky investment; we think your brother and sister can go much further in life."'

Recently Robert's father was being honoured by the local Rotary Club for ten years of membership in the organization, and for being the only Anglo-African in their branch. Robert's Mum said to Robert when he was getting dressed before the event, 'Do me a favour tonight at dinner, Robert. Don't give anybody that angry black look of yours. Try to be nice.'

Immediately, Robert said what he has said many times before. 'Mum, you are such a racist.' Just as quickly, his mother said dismissively, 'Yes, sure I am.'

Robert persisted. 'You really are a racist. I'm not joking.' His Mum cut him off and said, 'Just get dressed, Robert. And save your politics for college debates.'

When Robert came in for counselling the next week, he was furious with his mother. This incident had triggered a host of memories of times when Robert felt he had been treated as a second-class citizen by his own family. We had a long talk about how the internalized racism in Robert's family had caused his upwardly mobile relatives to underestimate Robert's potential, and to come down extra hard on him because of his darker skin and stronger features.

Then we discussed what might help his mother and father to understand just how painful it was to be on the receiving end of their dismissive racial comments. I asked Robert if he'd be willing to stop calling his parents 'racists' and start trying something more effective instead.

Robert argued, 'But they *are* racists. Why can't I just tell them the truth?'

I explained, 'It's easier to call our relatives a political label like "racist" or "sexist", but it only causes them to raise their eyes to heaven and ignore your legitimate concerns. What's harder but often more effective is to dig deep inside and be willing to let your family members see the unintended harm their words can cause. In order for this to work successfully, you will need to remind your Mum and Dad that you know they do care about you and that you assume they don't want to hurt you. You may need to admit to them that you're vulnerable and human. For many people, that's a much harder thing to say than to just blurt out the word "racist".'

Robert remarked, 'It's definitely a harder thing to say. I mean, why should I have to be the one to get vulnerable when my mother is saying hurtful things? She's the one who's wrong, and yet you want me to remind her that I know she loves me and doesn't want to hurt me.'

'That's exactly right,' I said. 'It's hard to stay loving and centred when you're facing the person who has just hurt you. But if you can do that and if you can remind your mother just how much she does care about you, then you've got a chance to penetrate her heart and get her to see why her comments about skin colour are so destructive and inappropriate.'

A few days later, Robert tried out what we had discussed. He took his mother to lunch at the weekend and said, 'I know you care about me and that you don't really want to hurt me. But when you or Dad talk about my skin and make it sound like I'm a lesser person than my brother and sister because of something I can't control, it hurts a lot. It makes me want to put up a wall and close myself off from the family, which is not what I really want to do. I've never been honest with you about this – about how hard it is for me. Please, Mum, you've got to think twice before you let my skin make you under-estimate who I am. It's not good for me as a person and it's not good for us as a family if you keep making decisions based on who's dark and who's light.'

To Robert's surprise, his words cut deeply into his mother's heart. He told me a few days after his conversation with his mother, 'I saw her face get really tense and I wasn't sure if she was going to be angry or defensive or what. But then I saw a couple of tears. My mother rarely gets vulnera-ble, but for a minute she looked at me with such love. It was as if she was seeing me, the real me, for the first time.'

If you decide to us this first approach of being vulnerable and clarifying exactly why the racist, sexist or homophobic remarks are hurtful to you personally, please be aware that your family member might still put up a wall. He or she might be unable or unwilling to face the fact that certain remarks can hurt someone unintentionally.

However, if you remind this person again that you know she does care about you and that you assume she doesn't really want to cause you pain, you will have a much better chance of breaking through the defensiveness and getting heard. I've found that even the most bigoted, intolerant and insensitive human beings have a heart, but in some cases it's covered with layers of emotional scar tissue and hardness. You will be taking a risk when you open up and admit your vulnerable feelings to this person, but it's the most powerful way to crack the layers of protection and defensiveness surrounding this person's fragile ego.

Find the good side of this person

A second approach that I have found works to break an impasse with intolerant or rigid relatives is what I call 'meeting them exactly where they are.' Here's how it works.

Instead of reacting against a particular viewpoint that you find offensive, why not accept that your family member is probably going to continue to hold this viewpoint, at least to some extent. Instead of trying to remake this person into a clone of you and your values, try to communicate with him in a way that's not threatening, and that shows respect for his deeper values and beliefs.

For instance, what if you or someone in your extended family is gay or lesbian and one or more of your relatives thinks that same-sex intimacy is forbidden by the Bible. Instead of trying to convince this family member to stop being religious or to ignore the teachings of his minister or spiritual teacher, what if you were willing to honour this person's religious values and at the same time to help him see a way to be more compassionate and accepting of the family member who is gay? This may sound hard to do, but I have seen huge breakthroughs in even some of the most dogmatic families using this approach.

'I don't want our family to be torn apart like this'

Elana's case is a good illustration of how to make this happen. Elana is a 40-year-old writer whose 17-year-old son, Ari, recently told the family that he is gay. Elana, who is Jewish, is reasonably comfortable with her son's sexual orientation, even though she worries about how he'll be treated in the wider world. She came in for counselling, however, because she has felt frustrated and upset at some of the remarks and reactions she's had from her older brother Sid, a conservative practising Orthodox Jew. On the day Elana made the counselling appointment, she had got into a shouting match with Sid, who told her, 'This is a *shanda* (a shameful scandal). You've got to do something to help Ari. It's not too late, and frankly you've been letting him act like a fag for far too long.'

Elana told me during her first session, 'It breaks my heart to see how this could split our family into factions. If push comes to shove, I will definitely side with my son, even if it means we stop having family get-togethers with Sid and his four children. But I don't want our family to be torn apart like this. Our parents were Holocaust survivors and we lost most of our relatives in the concentration camps. I love Sid, even though he can be a real pain sometimes.'

When I asked Elana what she hoped counselling might accomplish, she said, 'I wish I could get Sid to stop being so rigid in his beliefs. I wish I could say to my arrogant older brother, "Come on! It's the twenty-first century. Stop thinking and acting as if you're living in some narrow-minded Jewish ghetto in Europe a hundred years ago."'

Rather than encourage Elana to try to change Sid's religious convictions (which Elana told me was as likely to happen as the Pope appointing a Jewish cardinal), I asked her if she would be willing to respect Sid's beliefs even while helping him to be more compassionate. Elana said reluctantly, 'If I have to respect his beliefs, it won't kill me.'

So we began to discuss three ways to help a religiously observant Jew deal with these complex issues. First, I suggested to Elana that she help her brother to understand the dictionary definition of the word faggot, which refers to a bundle of wooden sticks burned as fuel. Some experts say this term originated in Europe in the Middle Ages when certain Christian clergy and civic leaders began tying up homosexuals and burning them in the town square. I said to Elana, 'After you explain the original meaning and history to Sid, see if he ever uses that hurtful word again, especially in light of your family's experiences in the Holocaust.' Quite often if you help a family member see the horrific history that underlies an insulting word he has been using casually, it will make him stop using it.

Second, I gave Elana a series of religious papers, articles and speeches put together by Rabbi Elliott Dorff, a highly respected Conservative scholar of Jewish religious law. Elliott Dorff has spoken out in favour of gay and lesbian rights and the need for gay and lesbian clergy. He and many others have argued that in light of research that shows the majority of gays, lesbians and bisexuals are trying to live up to their God-given way of expressing love and commitment, it would be wrong to judge or criticize them for it.

Elana said, 'I had no idea how seriously religious Jews were wrestling with such issues. I'd always thought that people who were traditional were just narow-minded, but now I wonder if I was wrong. There seem to be quite a few Jewish scholars and rabbis who are struggling to reconcile ancient teachings with modern thinking.'

Third, Elana and I explored together how much both traditional Jews like Sid and liberal Jews like Elana emphasize family closeness and the holiness of lifelong commitments. I asked her, 'Do you think Sid would be interested in being more flexible in order to keep your family together for special events each year? Do you think he would be willing to celebrate with you if Ari finds a life partner in the next few years and invites Sid and his family to a commitment ceremony conducted by a rabbi?' Elana's eyes filled with tears as she imagined the possibility of her brother celebrating her son's joyous occasion.

It took several weeks and a few stressful conversations before Sid shifted his stance and agreed to accept his nephew Ari. On the day when Sid finally invited Elana, Ari and the other relatives over for Sabbath dinner, Sid toasted his sister and his nephew and then said with a mischievous grin on his face, 'The past few weeks have been a bit of a miracle. First of all, yours truly became even more of a *mensch* (a good person). Second, I saw my liberal sister Elana sit down and study traditional Jewish texts, and she was even taking Jewish law seriously for once in her life. That's definitely a miracle. And finally, I got to know my nephew Ari much better than I ever have. He's a good person, and I'm grateful that his honesty and his courage have made this family stronger and closer than we've ever been.'

'We want our families to continue to love us'

A similar family dilemma that I encountered a few months ago involved a young woman, Ginger, who came to a talk I gave on dealing with family conflicts. Ginger is a 24-year-old sociology student who grew up in a Baptist family and discovered at the age of 22 that she was madly in love with a classmate, Amelia, who grew up a strict Catholic.

Unsure of whether or not to trust her strong feelings for Amelia, Ginger tried to pretend it was just a phase or a 'passing fancy'. She even talked to her family's minister, who warned her that if she acted on her desires she would be jeopardizing her salvation.

On the other hand, Amelia felt ready after a few months to move in together and make a commitment to Ginger. She had been comfortable with her own sexual orientation ever since her first crushes on girls at school and university. Amelia was worried, however, that Ginger might go back to a more conventional male/female relationship eventually. Ginger and Amelia were both anxious about rejection and bad feeling they might face from their families.

Then, after two years of trying hard to suppress her feelings and replace her romantic attraction for Amelia with involvement in the church, Ginger came across a passage in the Bible that made her cry uncontrollably. The passage said simply, 'And the truth shall set you free.'

Ginger told me, 'That Biblical passage made me realize that my truth has always been a spiritual desire to be in a committed loving relationship with a woman. My first crushes at school were towards girls I admired. I tried desperately to fancy boys and I even had a steady boyfriend for a year at school. But my deepest longing was to love a woman, and I decided the day I read those words in the Bible that it was time to stop pretending otherwise.'

As she had feared, this revelation caused an enormous amount of tension in her family. A few weeks later her Dad heard that she had been seen holding hands with Amelia in a restaurant. He immediately cut off her tuition payments and living expenses. Her mother called her a slut who would go to hell. Her older brother Ray tried to get her to see a 'conversion therapist' who attempts to reprogramme people to change their romantic feelings from one gender to the other.

In Amelia's family there was less drama, but she noticed 'a sense of coldness and distance had set in. My parents and my two sisters tried to act as if they were fine with my coming out, but you could tell they were very uncomfortable. At one point my younger sister said, "Why did you have to go and do this to Mum and Dad? Can't you see how disappointed they are?"'

During Ginger and Amelia's first counselling session, I had asked them, 'What is the best outcome you would want from this counselling?' Ginger and Amelia both agreed, 'We want our families to continue to love us.'

After spending several sessions exploring the tensions that each had experienced in her respective family, I asked Ginger and Amelia, 'What if I told you that we were going to have to take your family members' beliefs and discomforts seriously? What if I told you they might not ever feel fully comfortable with who you are?'

Ginger and Amelia looked at each other, and then Ginger said, 'We've talked a lot about how much we don't want to hurt our families. But we're also committed to being together and making a lifelong promise to build a healthy family, maybe even with one or two children. I suppose we're going to have to deal with our relatives exactly as they are and accept that this is going to be hard for many, if not all, of them.'

Amelia added, 'I love my family and I want them to accept and appreciate that I've found an amazing partner for life. But I have to accept that they may or may not be able to go against their fears that say Ginger and I are doing something wrong.'

Having accepted that their relatives might not change, Ginger and Amelia were now ready to talk to them heart-to-

heart. During the next few weeks, both women began discussing with each of their relatives how much they wanted
their family's love and how they knew this was not an easy
issue for any of them. I urged Ginger and Amelia to open up
the one-to-one conversations with each of their relatives by
saying in their own words what kind of closeness and mutual
respect they hoped for, even if their relatives were not able to
accept them completely.

Here's what Ginger said: 'I care about you and I want
you to know that I will always treasure the family closeness
we've had together. So please let me know whatever concerns
or questions arise because of what I've told you about who I
really am. I respect your feelings and your struggles with this.
Even if at times we're going to see things differently, I hope
we can do our best to treat each other like family and to learn
and grow from this.'

I also helped Ginger and Amelia find some articles,
speeches and other writings that explained how various
Protestant and Catholic clergy and scholars are addressing the
complicated issue of how to be a compassionate Christian
when dealing with family members and friends who are gay.
Specifically, I asked Ginger and Amelia to offer any of their
relatives who were interested a choice of three different written viewpoints on the issue: one from a minister who is convinced that homosexuality is an unforgivable sin; one from a
minister who is convinced that same-sex committed relationships are holy and sacred; and one from a minister who argues
strongly for church-sponsored gay and lesbian commitment
ceremonies and civil rights but is reluctant to support same-
sex marriages.

I told Ginger and Amelia, 'Let your relatives look over
these various points of view on the issue and know that each

of these Christian theologians takes the Bible and church tradition very seriously.'

It took a lot of courage and persistence for Amelia and Ginger to participate in these difficult discussions, particularly with some of their relatives. But over the next few weeks Ginger discovered that 'My family is a lot more diverse than I realized. My older brother Ray continued to insist he was horrified by my "sinful lifestyle choice" and hoped that I would reconsider. My aunt wanted to send me to a reprogramming camp where they try to convert people to heterosexuality. But my Mum and Dad shifted a little and were quite wonderful, saying, "We really appreciate how loving and courteous you've been in letting us show our feelings and concerns about this. It's not going to be easy, and we're anxious about your soul. But we'll always love you."'

Amelia described the situation in her family. 'There's still a lot of politeness and condescension. Most of my relatives say they're being compassionate, but really they just aren't willing to talk about how uncomfortable they are. And then there's my darling forthright grandmother, who said it best: "I'm going to let the priests and the scholars argue this one out. All I care about, Amelia, is that I thought you were a blessed gift from God the minute I saw you as a baby and I still think you're a blessed gift from God today. I can't wait to meet the lucky lady who will be spending her life with someone as spectacular as you!"'

If you show respect for your relatives' viewpoints by sharing books or articles on the issue so that they can decide for themselves how they want to deal with their mixed feelings, quite often this will encourage them to be a little more respectful of who you are as well. I can't promise success in every case, but I have seen that there can be warmth and mutual respect among relatives, even when there are strongly conflicting viewpoints over serious issues.

Investigate the psychology of the person's stance

When a family member rigidly refuses to loosen up about race, sexuality or gender issues, there's usually something deeper going on. Without condoning or making excuses for this person's insulting comments, I would urge you to do some detective work to find out why this person is so unforgiving on this particular topic.

For example, if you examine the family history and early childhood experiences of men and women who tell racial jokes or feel hostile toward people of different races, you will often find one of three possibilities.

First possibility: this person may have been taught some extremely negative and exaggerated stereotypes as a child. Now, as an adult, it's as though by telling racial jokes they are being loyal to the people or environment in which they grew up.

Second possibility: this person may have grown up in an insecure low-income household, or a formerly well-off family that was concerned about a fall in status, and so was told as a child, 'We're struggling to get by, but we're better than [a certain minority group].' Then, as members of that minority group began overtaking him on the road to success or happiness, resentment started to grow.

Third possibility: this person may have had a painful experience with someone from that race or ethnic group, or was told stories about someone else's painful experiences, and this one incident has become generalized into a lifelong fear or contempt for members of that group.

If you do some research by talking with your parents, grandparents, aunts, siblings, or cousins about the member of your family who tells racial jokes or makes racial slurs, you will probably find some useful information about how this person became so negative and hurtful. Once again, this research is not meant to excuse or justify his cruelty or insensitivity. Instead, it reveals the hidden wounds and beliefs that you will need to take seriously as you seek to discuss racial issues with this person.

'He just can't stop himself'

Camilla's case is an example of what can happen if you take time to consider the reasons why one of your relatives is bigoted or intolerant. A highly creative and intelligent woman in her early thirties, Camilla grew up in a family where the women wash all the dishes after a family meal while the men drink heavily and watch sport on television without lifting a finger to help. The sons are encouraged to pursue lucrative careers, while the daughters are warned that too much independence and outspokenness will frighten away potential husbands.

Camilla has always wanted to get closer to her father, a very complicated man who can be extremely kind and generous with strangers but very cold and authoritarian with his five children. He's especially harsh with Camilla, his eldest child, and he's been very critical of her attempts to establish her own life. He also tends to make insulting remarks about Camilla's imperfect figure, her imperfect cooking and her imperfect driving. When Camilla considered going away to college, her father insisted that she must stay close to home to take care of her younger siblings. When Camilla tried to start her own business as a graphic designer, her father refused to help her and told her she didn't know the first thing about money and would never succeed. When Camilla voices an opinion or disagrees with her father, he'll say, 'See, that's why you'll never get a husband.'

During our first counselling session, I asked Camilla how she responds to her father's comments. Camilla laughed and said, 'I eat chocolate. Or ice cream. My father is a sexist bastard, but for some reason I'm still trying to win his approval. Am I sick or what?'

After two counselling sessions in which we explored Camilla's business ideas and commitment to working hard to succeed, I asked her the following question: 'Do you feel as if you need your father's encouragement or do you think you will be able to succeed without it?'

Camilla was silent for a moment and then she said softly, 'I desperately want his encouragement and I'm terrified I'll never get it.'

That began a series of attempts to see if we could help her father recognize and acknowledge the hardworking and creative daughter he has. We tried approach number one, in which Camilla sat her father down and had a heart-to-heart talk about why his negative comments about women knowing nothing about business were holding her back. Her father listened impatiently and then said, 'You're just like your mother. Far too sensitive. That's going to hurt you in the business world. Mark my words.'

We tried approach number two in which Camilla tried to meet her father's standpoint regarding women and equality. She told him she appreciated that his overprotectiveness came from a loving concern to shield his daughters from the stressful ups and downs of life. She told him she would always be his little girl, even if she was successful in her graphics business. She also told him she loved him and hoped he would continue to be a crucial adviser she could always ask for help and support.

But after each of these attempts to get closer, Camilla continued to receive a cold look of disapproval from her father. Rather than her father reciprocating with warmth and encouragement, Camilla described his response this way: 'My father gets this distant look on his face as though he's feeling uncomfortable or is lost in his own thoughts. There I am, waiting like a stupid puppy for him to give me a bone, and he's sitting there all emotionally frozen. I hate him for it. At those moments I wonder if he's capable of loving me at all or if he's just stuck with a pushy daughter who isn't the kind of person he had hoped for.'

So Camilla and I decided it was time to do some research about why her father was so emotionally frozen and why he appeared to be unwilling to let down his guard with his eldest daughter. From talking with her paternal aunt and uncle, a few gems emerged. Camilla discovered from looking at one of her aunt's old photos of her father that when he was five years old there was a lightness and aliveness in his face that Camilla had never seen. But from the age of six, something changed.

According to Camilla's aunt and uncle, what happened when her father was six is that his own father died suddenly and his family suffered a severe financial setback. They had to move from a spacious country house to a tiny terraced house. Camilla's grandmother became a cleaner, working long hours cleaning up wealthy people's homes and taking care of their children. Camilla's father and his siblings were left at home under the supervision of his eldest sister, whom Camilla had never met.

According to the surviving aunt and uncle, 'Your father's eldest sister was not a safe person to be running a family. She was later diagnosed as seriously unstable emotionally, but at the time all we knew is that she was big and strong and had a very short temper. When your father was six years old and he used to answer back, she always beat him. The rest of us would avoid her anger, but your father tested her again and again. And each time she would get the better of him. It was horrible, and he kept it all inside. Your father has a lot of pride and he never wanted anyone to know about the beatings he was given by his 17-year-old sister. He would be furious if he knew we were telling you all this.'

As Camilla looked at the photos of her father when he was seven, eight, nine and ten, she saw his face looking more angry and withdrawn. The warmth and the lightness were gone from his expression and his eyes looked distant and sad.

Camilla realized that her father was probably still secretly intimidated or resentful towards any woman who spoke up assertively like his eldest sister. Yet as a result of these family stories, Camilla discovered her freedom. She knew for the first time in her life that she wasn't going to wait any longer for her father to change suddenly into a warm and supportive mentor. Nor could she hold her breath hoping her father would become comfortable with the idea of a woman being strong and independent.

The next time she was at her family's house for a meal, she looked with new eyes at her father. She no longer saw him as a bullying tyrant or a cruel person, but rather as a wounded individual who simply could not climb out of the protective shell he had put himself in long ago. She told me during a counselling session the week after the meal with her family, 'I sat looking at my father doing his "I'm the boss" routine and I said a silent "thank you" that I now knew what was going on inside him. I said to God, "Thank you for letting me see that my father's pain is not because of me but because of things that happened long before I was born. Thank you for helping me find a way to love him again, even if he doesn't have the ability to show his love for me"'

Over the next few months, Camilla's business began to grow and she also found herself in a good relationship with a man who grew up with a single Mum and has a lot of respect for strong women. During her final counselling session, Camilla told me, 'I still have a father who says some stupidly sexist nonsense. But his comments no longer hurt me the way they once did because I know they're more about his pain than about my being a successful and healthy woman.'

She continued, 'Every once in a while when I'm visiting my family, I can sense that my father does secretly enjoy the fact that my business is doing well and that I'm in a good relationship. He can't say it out loud because that would be admitting defeat, but I can see it in his eyes sometimes. There have been moments when I catch him looking in my direction and there's just the slightest glimpse of a smile on his worried and tense face. At those moments I know he loves me and I know that he respects me as much as he's ever been able to respect any woman. I'm lucky I waited to feel his love. It feels extremely good.'

CHAPTER NINE

WHAT IF THERE'S BEEN SERIOUS PHYSICAL OR EMOTIONAL ABUSE?

I s there someone in your family who has crossed the line from being just unpleasant to being actually abusive? Is there a family member who sometimes engages in psychological or emotional abuse, treating others in a cruel, vindictive or highly manipulative way? Is there someone in your family who has been physically violent or sexually inappropriate in the past and in whose presence you still feel uncomfortable as a result? As you think about your own family, consider the following cases:

> Moira is a 34-year-old fashion designer who has spent many years in therapy overcoming the psychological after effects of being molested by her father when she was ten years old. Fourteen months ago, Moira and her husband, Jay, had their first child and it stirred up a lot of confusion for Moira. 'I see all the other Mums having a break, letting their children spend time with loving grandparents, but I don't know what to do about my own family situation. Should I even think about letting my parents help with my daughter or should I keep them out of her life altogether?'

Alec is a 52-year-old widowed father of two grown-up children, one of whom is quite unstable emotionally. According to Alec, 'I love my son, but he's quite violent and out of control at times. A few years ago at Christmas he got angry about something and he smashed up several of my old photos and memorabilia. I haven't been willing to invite him to a family party since then, but I'm feeling a bit guilty. How long do I need to protect myself before I can reconnect with this troubled man who still needs a lot of support?'

Recently a woman named Iris came up to me after a speech I gave and said, 'I'm tired of hearing about ways to reconcile with difficult relatives. What if the family member is truly abusive? What if it's time to cut the ties with this toxic person?'

After hearing more about Iris's family situation, I thought about several of the clients I have seen over the years who have extremely abusive relatives and who asked this same thing: when is it time to cut yourself off from a truly harmful person? This is an important question that needs to be addressed carefully. On the one hand, it would be tragic if any of us were to abandon or refuse to help family members who are seriously mentally ill, substantially memory-impaired or chronically emotionally unstable. These relatives might be truly difficult, but they deserve patience and our best efforts to help them without burning ourselves out.

For instance, a member of my wife's family has been diagnosed with schizophrenia. At times he can be a wonderful person to be with, and he has a rich knowledge of jazz, blues, electronics and history. He understands the music of Miles Davis better than anyone I've met. Quite often he's humorous and loving. Yet at other times he says and does some very hurtful and harmful things. My wife Linda and I would never abandon him or stop doing what we can to help make his life better. We believe that being a part of a family includes taking care of those in the family who are unable to care for themselves.

On the other hand, there might be an abusive relative in your family who could get help to control his behaviour and yet refuses to do so. In situations where the abusive person poses a physical threat to you or another family member, the only healthy choice may be to distance yourself from this individual and to stop letting her disrupt every family event. There are also situations in which you have to admit your own human limitations and recognize that you might not be the right person to be the saint-like coach or constant probation officer for an abusive relative who has absolutely resisted any help you've offered. Sometimes the only healthy choice is to let the outside world give this abusive individual the harsh consequences he seems to invite.

But how do you know whether to hold on or to put some distance between yourself and a harmful relative? How do you work out when and how to protect the safety and sanity of the rest of the family? At some point it may come down to your establishing effective limits that say to the abusive family member, 'If you want to participate in family events, a certain level of behaviour is necessary. If you're not willing to abide by the basic rules of respect, then we're going to need to care about each other from a safe distance.'

In this chapter I provide you with specific questions and guidelines that can help you clarify the issues. How any limits get implemented, however, is up to you and your family members to work out together.

IS THERE A COVER-UP GOING ON IN YOUR FAMILY?

The first question for any family that has had to cope with someone's emotional cruelty, physical violence or sexually inappropriate behaviour is to ask, 'Have we uncovered the full extent of the problem yet? Or are we still trying to play down the situation or deny what really happened?'

Quite often when abuse has occurred or is occurring, people just don't want to face the full impact of what has been going on. It may be because family members are afraid or they are dependent on the very person who has been acting in an abusive way. If you try to get your relatives to address an abusive situation, especially one that has gone on for years, you might be accused of being too sensitive, fixated on the past, disloyal or worse. Yet the longer the family covers for the offending relative and keeps the abuse a secret, the more confusion and pain is likely.

For instance, Nicholas, 22, grew up with a hardworking but violent stepfather called Hal who often exploded in rages over the smallest incident. Nicholas has never been able to get his mother or his three older siblings to face what happened in their family. Nicholas explained, 'My two brothers and my sister were a lot older than me; they weren't living at home when my parents got divorced and my Mum got involved with Hal. So they just don't want to deal with what happened to me, trapped with an explosive person who knocked out two of my teeth and left scars on the back of my legs and bruises on my ribs.'

Nicholas continued, 'My mother witnessed much of it, but she's terrified of letting the truth come out because she doesn't want to lose Hal. Often I would tell my brothers and my sister that Hal had whipped me with a belt or beaten me with a tennis racket. They'd say, 'Oh, don't exaggerate. Mum says it never happened.' The problem has always been that Hal can be quite generous and kind. He's helped each of my siblings with their college tuition fees and he's always buying things for my Mum to keep her sweet. Hal is quite a charmer when he wants to be, but at any family party I feel sick trying to pretend we're one big happy family. My stepfather still gives me the creeps when he glares at me. I'm not the kind of person who can just pretend nothing happened over all those years.'

More than anything, Nicholas would like his mother and his other relatives to take him seriously and to stop covering for Hal. When Nicholas brought his mother and three siblings in for a family counselling session, it was difficult at first to get everyone to stop playing down what had happened between Nicholas and his stepfather. During the initial family session, Nicholas's older sister said, 'Oh, for crying out loud. You're being too sensitive This stuff, if it happened at all, took place a long time ago.'

Nicholas responded, 'But it's still happening. Just last month I got into a minor dispute with Hal about how often I need to change the oil in my car. Hal gave me that look of his and he said, "There you go being stubborn again. I ought to teach you a lesson." I don't know what that means, "teach you a lesson." Is it an empty threat or is he going to do something vicious again? There's no way I can be sure, and I don't feel much support from any of you on this.' For a moment it looked as though Nicholas was beginning to make some impact on his relatives. His eldest brother commented, 'I've seen that look in Hal's eyes. It's certainly scary, and maybe we need to back Nicholas up when he says Hal is starting to threaten him again.'

But Nicholas's mother quickly jumped in to play down each of the specific violent incidents that Nicholas claimed Hal had been involved with. 'Oh, you don't understand Hal,' she insisted. 'He's all bark and no bite.'

Then Nicholas said, 'Wait a second. I know I promised you, Mum, that I would never tell anyone what I'm about to say, but I can't keep your secrets any longer.' Nicholas then told his siblings that Hal had broken two of their mother's ribs a few years earlier. There was silence in the room for several seconds.

Nicholas's older sister asked their mother, 'Mum, is it true about Hal punching you during an argument and breaking your ribs?' Nicholas's mother looked down and said nothing. Then the sister repeated the question, 'Did it happen, Mum?'

'It only happened once,' she said.

The sister replied, 'We've got to make sure it never happens again.'

As a result of this chipping away at the family denial, the family members were now ready to unify for the first time and do something about the abusive situation that they had been ignoring for twelve years. I suggested they make a Family Protection Plan, which usually consists of three parts:

- First, what you will do *as a family* the next time your abusive relative says or does something inappropriate.
- Second, how you will *warn* the abusive relative about

what will happen if he or she does something threatening or harmful to anyone in the family.

- Third, what you will *say* to the abusive relative to make it clear you care about this person but you will no longer tolerate the abusive behaviour.

When Nicholas and his siblings heard this description of a Family Protection Plan, they began to brainstorm about how and when they would present their unified stance to Hal. Nicholas's mother seemed nervous about this sudden change in the status quo, but she kept silent as her four children joined together to make a plan to protect the family from future abuse.

After much discussion, this is the brief but powerful Family Protection Plan they developed:

1. If Hal said or did anything violent against Nicholas or anyone else in the family, the siblings were prepared to call the police and have him arrested.

2. This warning was going to be given to Hal by all of the siblings *together* in a family meeting the following week at my clinic.

3. The siblings were willing to say to Hal, 'We know you love our Mum and that she loves you. So if you successfully avoid making any threats of violence or any intimidating gestures towards Nicholas or the rest of us, then we'll do all we can to make sure you and Mum can continue to have a long-lasting relationship.'

The next week, Hal came to the family meeting. Nicholas and two of his siblings explained to Hal that they wanted future family gatherings to be positive and comfortable for each member of the family. They told him calmly and politely that violence or threats of violence would not be tolerated.

I could see that Hal was a little surprised at how unified and firm the siblings had become. Hal said, 'It looks like you all agree with each other. That's fine. But I don't appreciate the insinuation that I'm a violent person or that you have anything to fear from me.'

Then Hal paused and said, 'But if you want to make a deal that we'll have no more threats and no more bossing each other around, I can handle that. You're grown up now and I'll do my best to treat you that way.'

Nicholas's Mum was quite nervous during the entire session and didn't say much until the end. That was when she finally spoke up and said, 'Hal, I've never told you this because I care about you so much and I didn't want to hurt you. But you need to know that all those years when you were being too rough with Nicholas, I thought about ending our relationship. I hung on and I'm glad I did. But please don't ever do anything to push me into making a choice between my children and my husband. I love each of you and I don't want to lose the closeness with any of you.'

Then she looked at Nicholas for a moment and said, 'I'm sorry I was weak, and didn't stand up for you when you needed me to. You deserved better and I hope, one day, you'll be able to forgive me.'

Those were the words Nicholas had been waiting to hear for so many years. In Nicholas's case, he was fortunate that his siblings did unify with him to speak up and set limits towards the abusive family member. If Nicholas had not been able to get his older brothers and sister to join him in developing a Family Protection Plan, it might have been necessary for him to try one of two other options.

- First, he could have tried to enlist one or two family members who could back him up and be supportive allies even if his mother and other relatives refused to take his side. In many families all it takes is for one or two family members to appreciate your point of view regarding an abusive relative and the situation begins to feel a little less overwhelming. Even if several family members continue to be charmed or swayed by the abusive relative, you can feel strong and sane from having solid allies on your side.

- Second, Nicholas could have chosen to reduce his exposure to Hal and turn up for family gatherings only when Hal was not going to be there. In families where the majority of family members refuse to face the truth about abusiveness that has gone on for years, the next best option is to choose which individuals and which events are safe and to keep a distance from events where the abusive relative is likely to appear.

Even if the family holds it against you for keeping a healthy distance from the abusive individual, you have every right to take care of yourself. You can maintain your closeness with the healthy relatives in your family through phone calls, one-to-one visits and letters. You can respect your family by refusing to condone an unhealthy situation. In many cases, I have seen men and women maintain excellent relations with their relatives year after year, even if they chose to avoid the big family events. The goal is not to pretend you have a perfect family but to make the best of whatever closeness you can achieve with your non-abusive relatives.

For example, I have a professional colleague named Gloria who grew up having to deal with an extremely violent and verbally abusive older brother. When she was younger, Gloria used to cringe in fear because her troubled older brother often destroyed her dolls and teddy bears in gruesome ways. As an adult, her explosive older brother has on several occasions verbally attacked her and her children at family events. At a recent dinner, the older brother got into a shoving match with Gloria's youngest son and it looked for a moment as if things might get violent, until Gloria's huge uncle stepped in to stop her brother from going too far.

Gloria has tried for years to get her parents and other siblings to face the truth about how much her older brother needs psychiatric treatment and firm limits. Yet the family refuses to deal with the problem and thinks Gloria is being 'too sensitive'. As a result, for the past two years Gloria has arranged satisfying one-to-one visits with the members of her family that she enjoys seeing. She has skipped the family gatherings where her brother might be present. It's not perfect, but it has allowed Gloria to enjoy warm moments with the family members she loves and to avoid being victimized by the one family member who has threatened her. If this kind of situation sounds familiar to you, I recommend exploring with a counsellor or friend what your options might be for making the most of your quality moments with family and reducing your exposure to an abusive relative.

IS THERE A WAY TO STOP THIS INDIVIDUAL FROM DOING MORE HARM?

In many families where there have been abusive incidents in the past, limited contact with the offending relative is an ongoing possibility. For example, you might recall at the beginning of this chapter I mentioned Moira, a 34-year-old fashion designer whose father molested her when she was younger and who now has to decide whether or not to let her young daughter get to know her grandparents. Should she let her parents be involved with her daughter or not?

During her counselling sessions, I asked Moira what her gut instinct was telling her to do. She explained, 'There's a part of me that wants to say to my parents, "You bloody idiots. You ruined everything. You crossed the line and there's no way I'm going to trust you ever again." I can't trust my father because he's already proved he can be dishonest and selfish. And I can't trust my mother because for years she sided with him and tried to pretend I'd made the whole thing up.'

Then Moira paused and said, 'But there's also a part of me that remembers hundreds of fun moments growing up with my parents. My Dad used to love to take us boating and hiking and windsurfing. My Mum used to be so adorable when she'd sing to us or make us laugh with her silly faces.'

Like many people who have survived physical and sexual abuse, Moira felt naturally conflicting emotions. On the one hand, her parents had betrayed her trust in a manner that should never be allowed to happen. On the other hand, they were the only parents she has ever known, and deep inside she still cares about them.

Moira told me, 'I wish there were some way that my daughter could receive the love and doting that grandparents are supposed to give a young child. But how can I trust that they won't physically or psychologically do something that might harm her the way I was harmed?'

At this point in her counselling, Moira was ready to explore some realistic options that might allow her daughter to experience the love of grandparents while at the same time protecting her daughter against any form of abuse.

One option is to make sure your abusive relative is never out of your sight when he or she is with a vulnerable child. Another option is to insist that your abusive relative enroll in a course or programme for people who have crossed a harmful line. In some families that means your relative has to agree to take an extensive anger management course if he is going to be trusted to gain control over his explosiveness or violence. In other families it means he has to agree to take a course or programme in preventing child abuse or sexual abuse before he will be allowed to spend time with your child.

When I discussed these options with Moira, she said, 'I would feel satisfied if my parents took a course on preventing child abuse and if I could guarantee that they're never alone with my daughter. That means my husband or I need to be 100 per cent vigilant whenever my parents are around our daughter. Should they be allowed to babysit for us? Absolutely not. Should they be allowed to have private conversations that we can't see or hear? You're joking! Should I tolerate any strange comments or inappropriate tickling or touching? Not in a million years.'

A few weeks later we held a session with Moira's parents at my clinic. Moira explained these supervision ground rules to her mother and father. At first her mother was a bit defensive, saying, 'If you don't feel as if you can trust us, then why do you even want us to be near the baby?' Moira replied, 'Based on your history as parents, my instinct is to say you can't visit my daughter. But I'm thinking about my daughter's best interests. She deserves to have the love and affection of her grandparents – but only if the two of you are willing to abide by these rules.'

Moira's parents looked at each other, and then her father said, 'I think your suggestions are reasonable. I wish we could do more to help you out with babysitting because I know you've got a lot on your plate. But if supervised visits and a course in child abuse prevention is what needs to happen, it's worth it. I understand that you have every reason to be careful after what happened when you were younger.' Moira's Mum nodded in agreement. 'I just want to be able to spend time with my granddaughter. If supervision is what we need in order to make that possible, then that's what we need to do.'

After the session I spoke with Moira on the phone. Neither she nor I were sure whether her parents were telling the truth or saying what they thought we wanted to hear. When dealing with relatives who have proved to be self-centred or dishonest, it's often hard to tell when someone is being truthful or just manipulative. Despite her concerns, however, Moira told me, 'I'm taking my daughter over next Sunday to visit her grandparents. Wish me luck.'

In Moira's situation there was always some tension and distrust each time she or her husband watched her parents play with their granddaughter. According to Moira, 'I never was quite able to relax and say, "Oh, isn't this sweet." My mother and father might look to a naïve outsider like loving grandparents who would put a child's needs ahead of their own, but I know deep inside this is still somewhat risky. I expect to continue to monitor their visits closely as long as my daughter is young and vulnerable. I'd much rather be safe than sorry.'

In your own family, is there an abusive relative who might be able to improve his or her behaviour if watched closely? Or might there be some improvement if this person were to seriously engage in a course, programme or focused therapy to help overcome the attitudes and behaviours that made him or her so abusive in the past? Please note that I am certainly not suggesting you put yourself or your children at risk if you don't feel safe being near a relative who has proved already to be dangerous. Rather, the question is whether this dangerous person should be given another chance under very close supervision and very strict limits. Only you can make that choice.

IS IT TIME TO GET HELP IN DEALING WITH AN ABUSIVE FAMILY MEMBER?

Now we come to one of the toughest decisions that some families have to make. Even though we live in a society that says the family is a respected entity and we assume that each family should take care of its own members, nonetheless there are certain situations in which the family has to ask outsiders for help. If your abusive family member cannot stop being physically violent, sexually inappropriate or interpersonally exploitative, there may come a time when you need to say, 'Help! We can't resolve this on our own. We need people or resources that have more experience and better results with this kind of person.'

For example, if you are the parent of a teenager or young adult who is posing a physical danger not only to your family but also to others in the community, it may be difficult but necessary to ask local agencies and experts for help in finding the right programmes or services to prevent your teen or young adult child from doing more harm. Earlier in the chapter I mentioned Alec, whose young adult son had an anger problem. Alec found that his son was unwilling to accept any advice from him. Yet his son did make some progress when Alec paid for him to attend a seven-week programme on anger management.

Knowing your limits and asking for outside help are crucial steps in resolving many other family dilemmas as well. If you are a sibling or spouse of someone with severe mood swings who sometimes crosses the line into verbal or physical abuse, you may need to start making phone calls to find the right healthcare professionals to help your loved one. In many cases, the person can be helped with medication, psychotherapy or support groups. The trick is finding the right professionals who can be both polite and firm with your loved one.

Or if you are the adult child of a mentally impaired elderly parent who is posing a physical danger to others or to herself, you will need to start investigating how to keep your parent from doing harm. Or if you are in touch with a family member of any age whom you know is planning to do something destructive and this could be prevented, you have a responsibility to act.

In each of these cases, the challenge is to make sure you do the right thing and not sit on your hands or wait for your worst fears to come true. I strongly recommend that if you suspect that your troubled family member is at all close to harming to anyone, including himself, you quickly contact local agencies for guidelines on how to take appropriate steps to prevent a tragedy from happening. Quite often close relatives are among the first to know that something isn't right with a loved one who is crossing the line into violence or harmful behaviours. It's your job to find out quickly how to keep your abusive relative from becoming – or producing – another crime statistic.

What's the right thing to do?
Imagine for a moment that you were the sibling of Theodore Kaczynski, the isolated but brilliant man who sent long,

rambling notes and letter bombs to university professors. If you were watching the news and you began to suspect that your brother might be the notorious Unabomber, what would you do? Would you hope your gut instinct was wrong or that the problem might go away if you ignored it? Would you try to help your troubled sibling avoid capture? Or would you do what the actual brother, David Kaczynski, did to prevent numerous deaths? He turned in his own brother to stop him from doing any more harm.

A less dramatic dilemma faced by many families is what to do if you suspect that a member of your family is bullying, neglecting or verbally damaging another family member. It might be a frustrated adult carer who is starting to become abusive to an elderly relative who cannot protect herself. Or it might be a short-tempered parent whom you suspect is being verbally abusive or physically cruel to a child whose behaviour pushes this parent too far.

What is the right thing to do if you have strong clues that there is child abuse or elder abuse occurring in your own family? In order to make this decision, there are three facts you need to bear in mind.

- First, it has been shown repeatedly that those individuals who are being abused feel betrayed not only by the abuser but also by the family members who remained silent or helped to cover up the abuse.
- Second, if suspected cases of child abuse or elder abuse are not reported, the abuse tends to continue and get worse, while the perpetrator often moves on to harm other individuals as well.
- Third, no one that I've ever spoken to has ever said she felt comfortable or 100 per cent certain when making

a call to the appropriate agencies about child abuse or elder abuse. In fact, even when you have substantial proof that abuse or neglect is occurring, you will still have queasy feelings, or want to close your eyes and pretend you don't know what you do know.

I hope you never have to make such a painful choice, but if you suspect that your abusive relative is about to do something that could cause injury or death to innocent people, I urge you to do everything you can to keep your family member from bringing pain and suffering to other families.

'She's got the patience of a floor trader on speed'

One of my clients is Lucy, a potter in her late fifties who recently told me about a painful decision she had to make. She had visited her elderly aunt Chloe, who suffers from Alzheimer's disease and is being cared for by her eldest daughter, Lucy's cousin Eileen. During the visit, Lucy noticed several signs of neglect. Her aunt was sleeping in soiled underwear and had scratch marks and sores on her arms and legs. Lucy also overheard Eileen, a chronic drinker with a short fuse, screaming at Chloe, calling her a 'witch', a 'nightmare', a 'monster', and an 'idiot'.

As Lucy told me, 'I was horrified to see how nasty the situation had become in just a few months. I always knew Eileen was a bit intense. Her younger brother, who works for an investment banking company, said of Eileen, "She's got the patience of a floor trader on speed." But I had no idea she was stepping over the line and mistreating her own mother.'

I discussed with Lucy two options for doing the right thing in a situation like this. I said, 'We can call the police and they'll investigate, but we won't know whether the police officer is experienced in such complicated situations or not.

Or we can call a charity such as Age Concern that specializes in this kind of dilemma; they'll help make ensure that Eileen doesn't continue to be left alone with her Mum. And we can work with them to organize a better carer situation for Chloe and her family.'

Over the next few days, several things happened. Lucy contacted a charity that sent a caseworker to evaluate the situation. She also phoned several of Chloe's other relatives and arranged a family meeting with the caseworker. At the family meeting we came up with several options for improving Chloe's care, and for helping Eileen learn more effective ways of dealing with a relative who has Alzheimer's. Specifically, the caseworker and the family made the following Family Protection Plan.

1. Eileen was going to have to take a course in caring for the elderly and be monitored by a caseworker before she would be allowed to be alone with Chloe again.

2. Eileen's younger brother, along with Lucy and two other cousins, agreed to start paying what each could afford on a monthly basis to cover trained nursing care to help Chloe. They also agreed to start looking for a safe and clean nursing home in case Chloe's home care became too expensive or difficult.

3. Eileen's younger brother was asked to handle some of financial matters that had been especially stressful for Eileen.

4. Lucy agreed to make a few phone calls each week to remind aunts, uncles, cousins and old friends that Chloe still needed visitors and that she still was able to appreciate conversations and acts of kindness.

What started out as a tragic abuse situation turned into a breakthrough for Chloe and her extended family. It didn't cure the Alzheimer's. Nor did it turn Eileen into Mother Teresa. Eileen continued to be somewhat aggressive and impatient, but far less so than before she went on the course and got support from other relatives.

Yet it took Lucy sticking her own neck out and making some difficult phone calls before the abusive situation began to improve. I urge you to make sure in your own family that you bring in knowledgeable outsiders for help and advice. Your job is not to repair overnight long-standing personality clashes and abusive behaviours in your family, but if the situation calls for it you should be prepared to bring in people who can help – one step at a time.

CHAPTER TEN

HOW TO MAKE SURE FUTURE GENERATIONS WILL HAVE AN EASIER TIME

Now we enter the final chapter of this book. You may have thought when you first started reading chapter one that you were learning about how to deal with difficult relatives only in order *to help yourself*. But ten chapters later, you may have discovered that this topic of difficult family members is about much more than preventing your own indigestion or tension headache at the next family gathering. This book has also been about preventing the kinds of mistreatment and miscommunication that damage our families and our world. It's about healing not only one's self but generations to come.

In this final chapter I will focus on four specific things you can do to increase the likelihood that your children, your grandchildren, your nieces, your nephews and others will benefit from your insights and your positive steps towards improving things in your family. You will hopefully become one of the agents of change that help to make things better for those who will seek healthy closeness at both large and small family gatherings in the future.

What are the steps you can take starting right away to make your family atmosphere more nurturing and less upsetting for the next generation? Here are a few specific actions that have worked for many of my clients.

ACTION ONE: DO WHAT YOU CAN TO BREAK AT LEAST ONE HARMFUL FAMILY PATTERN

In each chapter of this book we've explored a different irritating trait that one or more of your relatives may have brought to family meetings. Now comes the chance to choose at least one of these traits that you are committed to stopping or not repeating. For example, you might choose to refrain from criticizing family members about their weight, income, sex roles or marital status, as some of your relatives have. You might choose to be the first one who says to the members of the next generation, 'It's fine to be who you are and not tie yourself up into knots trying to win family approval.'

Maybe you will be the first member of your family to stop criticizing the mistakes and imperfections of others and to start responding to your relatives with more compassion and sensitivity. Maybe you will be the first of your relatives to stop using sarcasm or condescension at family gatherings. Or maybe you will be the first member of your extended clan to appreciate and welcome into the family those outsiders who have been judged, gossiped about and rejected for far too long. Or maybe you will be the first adult in your family to be a helpful mentor to one or two members of the next generation – instead of being wrapped up in your own interests.

Pruning the family tree

What is the one specific trait or behaviour that you are interested in pruning from the family tree? Only *you* can decide. But imagine if each of the healthy members of your family did this as well. What would the future be like if they weren't saddled with the same harmful family patterns as you?

'Everyone in our family is always "too busy"'
Here's a brief example of how making a commitment to being an agent for change can help you focus on one family trait you want stopped. Mary is a 42-year-old client who works long hours as a designer for television shows. According to Mary, 'I grew up in a family where everyone was usually too busy to set aside much time to be together.' Mary's father is an entrepreneur who still works seven days a week at his various businesses. Her mother is a teacher and mystery book writer who usually is too busy to spend much quality time with her family. Her older sister is a medical researcher and university professor who hasn't taken a proper day off or a non-working holiday for years. Her younger brother is a computer games designer whose company seems to think that working 'part-time' means a 60-hour week.

As Mary admitted, 'It seems as if everyone in our family is always "too busy". We always say we'd like to spend more time with one another, but it never happens. And I'm realizing that my niece and nephew are growing up without my spending much time with them. It's sad because I don't have children of my own and yet I'm always too busy to really connect with these two. I wish I could find the time to be a positive influence on them and maybe even to offer them some less-stressful options than their relatives and I have taken. But every week I'm under so many deadlines at work I just never get around to setting aside time with them. Pretty soon six months have passed and they've changed beyond recognition again. It's so sad that all the adults in their life are too busy to truly connect with them.'

During one of our sessions I asked Mary, 'How would you like to be the first member of your family to make a commitment to the next generation – to get past being "too busy" and actually spend some quality time with these young-sters who need a healthy sounding board about life and diffi-cult choices?'

Mary's face lit up for a moment. 'I would love to make my niece and nephew a bigger priority than they have been.' But then she thought for a moment and commented, 'Except I am so swamped with work at the moment. How can I fit it in?'

I told Mary what I have told many of my clients who were unsure of how to find time for quality family moments. I said, 'It starts with a commitment in your heart and then just a small amount of time firmly set aside from your daily and weekly schedule. I'm not talking about quitting your job or becoming a different person. I'm talking about making a conscious choice to ensure these children remain an impor-tant part of your life.'

Mary began spending half an hour a day on the phone talking with these two and just a few hours each weekend enjoying one-to-one time with her niece and nephew. As she said several months later, 'It was the most rewarding choice I've ever made. Just a couple of hours each week taking my niece to museums and to her hockey matches, or driving my nephew to his music lessons and rugby practice, has made a huge difference. We talk about all sorts of stuff in the car and when we stop for ice cream or lunch. Every few weeks I notice that something I've said or done has influenced the way they think or make choices.'

Mary added, 'Sometimes I talk to my niece and nephew about why there's so much pressure in our extended family to work so hard and be so success-orientated. These two completely agree, telling me exactly how it feels to live with two workaholic parents and so many to-do lists. They love having someone they can open up with, someone who appreciates them unconditionally, and I'm very lucky to be able to give them the gift of being a family member who cares. I wish someone in my family had been willing to spend time with me when I was younger and just talk to me like a person. It's the kind of family closeness I've always wanted but have never been able to achieve.'

ACTION TWO: USE FILMS AND BOOKS TO HELP SORT OUT WHAT'S HEALTHY AND WHAT'S NOT

An extremely useful thing you can do to help future generations of your family make positive choices in life is to debrief them about the issues they will need to resolve in order to become sane adults. I have found as a therapist that films, books, magazine articles, songs and short stories are often effective ways to spark conversations about family issues that need addressing. These different means of expression become safe vehicles for talking about what's never previously been said.

You may need to do some research to come up with a book, short story or magazine article that touches on the specific issues that relate to your family. Then you could suggest sitting and eating popcorn with your younger relative while the two of you watch and discuss a rented video or DVD that has parallels to the family issues he or she faces. All you have to say is, 'I'd love to hear what you think,' and you'll be amazed at what children will tell you.

Finding the right resources

But where do you find the right films, books, articles or stories to spark such healing conversations with your children, grand-children, nieces, nephews or other relatives? I recommend asking librarians, bookshop staff, video shop staff, English teachers and others who can point you in the right direction. Or look on the internet, especially under major bookselling sites like Amazon, for their recommended books on a particular subject.

To give you just one idea, I recently asked some therapists and family experts to suggest films about dysfunctional families. There was a wide range of films; here are a few examples that might be useful for your own family conversations:

> *Divine Secrets of the Ya-Ya Sisterhood* – Based on two novels by Rebecca Wells, this is a good film to watch if you want to experience both revulsion and empathy toward a self-absorbed parent. It explores how the unfinished business of your parents' marriage can affect your own adult life and relationships.

> *Affliction* – Adapted from Russell Banks's novel, this Paul Schrader film with Nick Nolte and James Coburn is a painful look at how growing up with an abusive, alcoholic father can scar someone and alienate him from the people who care for him.

> *American Beauty* – This is a disturbing look at a man who hates his suburban life and can't communicate with his status-obsessed wife or his alienated, unhappy teenage daughter. Several experts called this the most dysfunctional family ever filmed.

> *My Big Fat Greek Wedding* – You don't have to be Greek to appreciate Nia Vardalos's comedic look at how

cultural differences, sexism and a tradition-orientated father can affect a first-generation immigrant family.

Terms of Endearment – From Larry McMurtry's novel about a mother and daughter who are so emotionally intertwined it hurts.

Ordinary People – Based on Judith Guest's novel and directed by Robert Redford, this movie shows the kind of lingering guilt, sadness and rigidity that can affect family members differently following the death of a beloved child.

In addition to these well-known films, here are some other ideas from the survey and from my counselling experience. Several therapists and family experts recommended rewatching *Cinderella* as a great way to stir up insights and feelings about what it's like to be a neglected stepchild in a family where jealousy and competitiveness are prevalent.

If there is someone in your family with a severe mental illness and the other siblings want a film that can help explore their own reactions to the ups and downs of living with such a troubled individual, I recommend *Dominick and Eugene*, which starred Ray Liotta and Thomas Hulce. If you have a family member who creates havoc because of his or her drug addiction, the other family members will probably benefit from watching and talking about the film *Ulee's Gold*; written and directed by Victor Nunez, it stars Peter Fonda as a bee-keeper and devoted parent who raises his son's children and somehow finds a way to maintain his dignity and stability despite painful family disruptions. For a film that will spark conversations about adoption, sexual abuse by a sibling, or resilience despite a troubled childhood, I recommend the film *Antwone Fisher*, which was directed by co-star Denzel Washington.

Finally, there is one other film that I have suggested to many of my clients who were trying to help younger family members understand why family gatherings are so stressful and conflict-prone. The film is called *What's Cooking?* and it came out in November 2000. It reveals how a Thanksgiving dinner brings out the best and the worst in four families – Jewish, Vietnamese, Latino and African American – who live in Los Angeles. Prepare to laugh and cry, as you will see your own family stresses played out on the screen. No matter where your family comes from, it should give you a lot to talk about.

ACTION THREE: POINT OUT THE MEDICAL, FINANCIAL AND PSYCHOLOGICAL CHALLENGES INHERENT IN YOUR FAMILY

You would be amazed at how many families never really talk about practical matters. The children and grandchildren are simply expected to work it all out by themselves, and as a result they often feel confused or resentful about the challenges and opportunities that are quietly but surely passed down from their older relatives.

Airing the family closet

Every family has some skeletons in the closet that we wish the next generation wouldn't discover. But the subconscious mind is always trying to work out what is hidden or unspoken. Quite often when someone comes in with a long-term compulsion or unhealthy pattern of financial, sexual or psychological behaviour – I would say in at least 30 per cent of cases – there is a family secret or hidden story that needs to be understood before the compulsion can be overcome.

Furthermore, ailments such as late-onset diabetes, food allergies, ulcers and other digestive disorders could be prevented
or lessened if people talked about these risks early enough.

The following list suggests some helpful ways to clear
the air and fill in younger relatives on family traits to watch
out for:

- If your family has secrets, sends mixed messages or
  struggles with control issues about money and inheri-
  tances, could someone possibly talk about these taboo
  subjects sooner rather than later, so that younger relatives will have a better grasp of the financial challenges
  they will be facing?

- If your family is well off, have you or anyone else ever
  talked honestly about some of the unfortunate side
  effects of having money, such as lack of motivation,
  focus or perseverance, that can affect future heirs?

- If your family has relatives who've done time in prison,
  been involved in feuds with other family members,
  had affairs that have been kept hush-hush or who have
  children from other relationships, wouldn't you rather
  these stories come out in a calm conversation that you
  initiate at the right time than wait until a version gets
  shouted out in anger or bitterness at the most awkward moments?

- Has your family ever talked about psychological problems that run in your family – such as depression, anxiety, panic attacks, bipolar disorder or drug and alcohol
  dependency – as these should be looked out for and
  dealt with properly.

- Has anyone in your family ever sat down and
  explained to younger members of the family why cer-

tain relatives don't get on or why a specific relative is so unpleasant some of the time and so loving at other times?

- Has there ever been a conscious effort made to explain to the next generation in age-appropriate ways the heroic or courageous things that some of their ancestors did under challenging circumstances?
- Have you ever made time to discuss with your younger relatives the good and bad things about being a man or a woman in this family, or what it means to have the racial, ethnic, religious or cultural issues that exist in your family?
- Do your relatives talk openly about your family's medical history and the risk of heart problems, high blood pressure, breast cancer or any other hereditary illnesses that should be looked out for?

Most people are happy talking about trivia, but they may be uncomfortable talking about the real issues that affect their family. What if instead of hiding the truth from the next generation you pointed out things they will need to know in order to cope better with life?

'I wish someone had just told me the truth'
A few years ago I counselled Matthew, a man in his fifties who had spent much of his life making unfortunate choices in relationships. He told me, 'For some reason I'm just not attracted to women who are down-to-earth and reliable. I always seem to be captivated by the unpredictable, self-obsessed and fiery ones.'

As a result, Matthew had been married and divorced three times. Each time he found himself pursuing yet another unpredictable and unstable relationship. According to Matthew, 'It's been expensive because I care about these women and I support them and the four children who have resulted from these messy relationships. I would hate to make the same mistake again, but I still find myself drawn to women whom my friends warn me are trouble.'

During one of our sessions, I asked him, 'What were you told about your parents' marriage, and what does your gut instinct tell you their marriage was like?'

Matthew described how his parents had been married for more than 55 years and claimed to have a successful marriage, even though he has always wondered if there was something more they weren't telling him.

I asked Matthew, 'What do you think they've never told you?'

'I don't know,' he said.

So I asked Matthew to do some research and ask his aunts and uncles what they knew about the early years of his parents' marriage. A few weeks later, Matthew came into my office and said, 'You're not going to believe what I found out. According to one of my aunts, my mother was not always the cake-baking and school committee Mum I knew.

'When I was two years old, she supposedly had this passionate affair with her boss from the ad agency where she used to work. He promised he would divorce his wife and Mum was going to get a divorce, too, so they could get married. But it never happened, and within a few years my mother had become the quiet and repressed woman I knew for all those years.'

Matthew looked at me with an expression of relief and openness I had never seen in him before. He commented, 'If someone had sat me down when I was eighteen years old and explained to me the complexities of who my mother is and what their marriage has been like, I feel as though this huge mystery would have been lifted from me. I wish they had told me the truth. I could've handled it and I don't think I would have spent all these years trying to find the wild woman I was somehow going to rescue.'

You may think you're doing the next generation a favour by glossing over the real stories about their relatives, but they need to understand. You may think it's ancient history or too private to discuss, but I hope you will find the right time and place to bring these secrets to light. Only when your younger relatives have full access to the family history can they make sense of what happened long ago and how to change it in the future.

ACTION FOUR: WHY NOT BRAINSTORM WITH THE NEXT GENERATION TO RESOLVE FAMILY DILEMMAS?

In many families people are reluctant to talk with their children and grandchildren about family dilemmas. For example, if someone in the family has a serious illness, adults often try to hide this from the children. The children know something is going on, but instead of being told the truth they get evasive replies to their questions that make them feel suspicious or confused. Or, when there is a financial crisis the children might want to know why their parents are so tense. Instead, the adults bend over backwards trying to hide the truth, so the kids surmise that something horrible is going to happen or that the adults are angry with them about something. Or the adults will pretend that money isn't a problem but then snap angrily at their children for wanting to buy something.

Identifying the elephant

Instead of trying to hide the elephant that everyone suspects is walking around in your family, sit down with your children, grandchildren, nieces or nephews and say, 'We need to have a family meeting about something important that is affecting all of us. We need your ideas and suggestions on how each of us can handle this situation better than we've been doing so far.' The following example illustrates the value of including your younger family members in the equation when dealing with problems.

'We didn't think it would be fair to burden them with this'

I recently counselled a married couple who were extremely stressed because the wife, Ingrid, had been diagnosed with multiple sclerosis and the husband, Bernard, was about to be made redundant. Despite the huge personal and financial pressures they were facing, Ingrid and Bernard had tried to pretend in front of their three kids that everything was fine. As Ingrid explained, 'We didn't think it would be fair to burden them with this. We don't want them to worry.'

But when the three children came in for a session, we found out that they were well aware that Mum and Dad were acting strangely. The 17-year-old daughter, Alicia, said, 'Mum has been so short-tempered lately. I feel as if whatever I do she finds fault with.' The 14-year-old sister, Ginnie, commented, 'My parents keep having these whispered conversations behind closed doors. All three of us are convinced they're about to get divorced.' The youngest in the family, 10-year-old Phillip, remarked, 'I think Mum and Dad don't want to be our parents any more. They just seem to be far too busy lately. I think they're going to ask us to go and live at our aunt's house, which would be a pain because it's four miles away and none of my friends would be allowed to ride their bikes that far to visit me.'

None of the children knew why things were so tense, but they all sensed that something huge and dreadful was going on. As you will find in families that keep secrets, children often imagine scenarios that are much worse than what is actually happening.

At the next session with just Ingrid and Bernard, I asked, 'Do you still feel you want to keep your illness, and your redundancy secret from your children?' Ingrid was silent for a moment, and she looked at Bernard to see his reaction. Bernard put his hands over his face and said quietly but firmly, 'The children should *not* be told.'

I waited for a few moments and then said, 'I want to respect your wishes. But could you explain why you feel so strongly about this?'

Bernard remained silent as Ingrid said, 'This is a huge issue for Bernard. When he was sixteen his father became seriously ill with an incurable disease. All of a sudden, Bernard was no longer allowed to be an innocent child having fun or enjoying life. His parents insisted he get a job and help support the family. He also had to help his mother raise the three younger siblings. And he had to watch his strong and independent father rapidly decline and become physically dependent through his terrible illness.'

Bernard continued to sit in silence and Ingrid added, 'I feel as though my husband has carried a huge load of resentment and pain inside him because he was forced to grow up so suddenly. That's why he is so moody and difficult at times. And I'm afraid my being diagnosed with MS is going to make him feel overwhelmed and resentful.' During the rest of that session, I explored with Bernard what it had been like as a 16-year-old having to suddenly carry so much. I wouldn't say that Bernard was exactly talkative, but he did reveal his greatest fear: 'That my own three children would lose their childhood and always resent us for it.'

As with most psychological issues, there was some basis for Bernard's worries, but there were also some inaccurate perceptions. I said to Ingrid and Bernard, 'I agree that it would be unfair and harmful if you suddenly demanded that your children rush in and try to save the family from the illness and the financial pressurees that are more than a child could handle. I completely understand that you don't want to force them to surrender their innocence and their childhoods because of these huge new challenges in your family.'

Yet I also suggested, 'There's another way of looking at this situation. If you sit down with your children and treat them respectfully as intelligent and caring individuals, you can ask for their ideas and suggestions on what they feel they would like to do to to help and what they think would be unfair or excessive. If you reassure them that you value their intelligence and that their opinions are important, you might be surprised at how they will come up with some options that balance the need to help the family and the need to have a childhood.'

At first, Bernard was sceptical. 'Do you really think they're old enough to be able to understand what's going on?'

I replied, 'I don't know for sure. They're your children and you know them a lot better than I do. But in my experience, if you ask a 17-year-old, a 14-year-old, and a 10-year-old for suggestions on how to help during a family crisis while making sure they still have their normal routines and pleasures, you will be amazed at how many good and practical ideas they'll come up with.'

Ingrid looked at her husband and said, 'Bernard, trust me. Of course I want them to have a childhood, but I really believe this could be a chance for them to feel we respect them and their contributions to the family.'

Bernard thought without speaking for almost a minute, and then he finally replied. 'I'm not convinced, but I'll give it a try.'

So at the next session, I invited the whole family to start working together and brainstorming about what each of them could do to make things easier in view of the medical and financial stresses they were facing – and to make sure there was still time and energy for doing the things each of the children enjoyed doing most. This was the beginning of a huge change in how this family operated. For the first time the children were being given a crucial role in problem solving and family teamwork. For the next hour, each family member came up with several good ideas on how they could stay balanced while also doing their bit to help respond to the current crisis.

The middle child, Ginnie, offered to cook meals and let her Mum rest more, but she also said that she wouldn't be able to cook on Tuesday or Thursday nights when she had gymnastics classes. The eldest daughter, Alicia, said she was willing to take a part-time job as a bookkeeper for her aunt's business to help her parents financially, but that she still wanted to keep Friday and Saturday nights free for going out with her boyfriend. The youngest child, Phillip, offered to take out the rubbish each week, clean up the kitchen once a day and do his homework each night without his parents having to beg him; but he added, 'I still want to be able to watch my favourite programmes on TV for one hour each day and three hours on weekend mornings,' to which Ingrid replied, 'Two hours maximum at weekends.' Phillip smiled as he said, 'I thought I could get one past you, Mum, but you're still pretty sharp.'

As part of the family brainstorming, Ingrid offered to join a weekly MS information group so that she could keep up with the best strategies for managing her illness. She also told her children, 'I want to make sure I'm still involved in your daily homework and your everyday decisions. Don't think that just because I'm not well there's no one here watching you.' Bernard promised to spend at least three hours a day looking for a new job and one hour a day working out at the gym to make sure he didn't slip into depression.

Rather than being a shameful burden, the family stresses became an opportunity for these five individuals to rally together. It became a chance for the next generation to learn about teamwork, balance, good communication and mutual respect.

I have found in numerous families that once the members stop hiding from the truth and instead call upon each individual to brainstorm on what can be done, it almost always strengthens the family. These family brainstorm meetings can be especially effective if you make it clear from the start that you want each family member to stay balanced and avoid burning out – to do a lot to help the family but also to keep time and energy for his or her individual needs and pursuits.

As Ingrid said a few months after this brainstorming session, 'I'm sorry it took MS and redundancy to make my family closer and more loving than ever. But these past few months have been an unexpected blessing because I see all three of my children developing parts of their personalities they never had to tap into before. It's been a frightening time for our family, and yet I'm seeing that each of my children is growing up with a good feeling for how to respect his or her own needs while helping others. That's something I wish I'd learned as a child.'

LOOKING FOR PROGRESS, NOT PERFECTION

As with many of the cases in this book, I hope you recognize in the above example that when it comes to family dilemmas there are rarely perfect solutions or painless options. In most family situations there will always be some complicating factors and some difficult relatives to keep things interesting. The family meeting didn't cure Ingrid's multiple sclerosis, but it did allow her to feel the strong family support that's necessary for her ongoing care. The brainstorming session didn't suddenly turn Bernard into an outgoing, fun-loving individual, yet it did help him see that his children were a lot happier and more balanced than he had thought they would be, in spite of his job situation.

I cannot promise you that after reading this book your family stresses will disappear. Instead, I predict that your narcissistic relatives will still be self-absorbed and your impulsive relatives will still be impulsive. But isn't that the beauty of being part of a family? Even with all the conflicts and disagreements, there can be deep caring and commitment.

Yes, there will still be moments when you look around at a family gathering and you say to yourself, 'My goodness, am I strong enough to survive these people?' There will still be times when you mutter under your breath, 'Why does this particular person have to be so difficult year after year after year?'

I wish you and your loved ones strength and courage as you deal with the ups and downs that take place in your immediate and extended family. I hope you have many moments of closeness and celebration with the relatives you enjoy as well as fewer moments when your most difficult relatives get on your nerves. Please don't forget that dealing with family issues is a lifelong process of learning and discovery. But it's definitely worth the effort, as future generations will be better off because of each step you take to improve the level of respect and compassion among your relatives.

Remember, the goal is not to have a perfect family but a sense that, with each passing year, you make some progress in how you connect with these complex people who are a crucial part of your journey in life.

ABOUT THE RESEARCH STUDY

For more than twenty years I've been conducting workshops at UCLA Extension and other adult education programmes for men and women of all ages dealing with their difficult relatives. At these events I often get asked, 'What percentage of people have difficult relatives and family conflicts?'

Usually the person asking the question admits that he or she feels somewhat alone in having family clashes or expects he or she is part of a small percentage of people who have serious family stresses year after year. I've noticed that most individuals assume the majority of families are well behaved or harmonious; most people are concerned or embarrassed that their particular family has feuds, tensions or personality clashes.

I knew I couldn't answer the question 'What percentage of people have difficult relatives and family conflicts?' just based on my clinical psychotherapy practice or the unrepresentative sample of individuals who sign up for workshops on family dilemmas. So several years ago I began looking to see if there were any scientific studies or research that might address this issue. I never found a statistically valid scientific study. I decided to conduct a carefully designed research study of over 1400 randomly selected men and women to find out just how rare or common these family tensions tend to be. My hope was to interview a realistic and statistically valid nationwide sample across all races, ethnicities, ages, income groups and family backgrounds that would give us a good estimate of just what goes on behind closed doors in our immediate and extended families.

The design. A statistically significant research sample of over 1400 people were randomly selected and asked the following questions.

1. Do you have just two minutes for a quick survey? All answers will be kept private and confidential.
2. Do you have any immediate or extended family who get together for holiday meals, birthday meals or other family events?
3. How would you describe your family holiday events and get-togethers?
   a. Enjoyable
   b. Sometimes enjoyable, but sometimes very difficult
   c. Rarely enjoyable, but an obligation I do anyway
   d. We don't get together because of (death, geography, tensions, no one initiates)
4. Is there someone in your immediate or extended family who gets on your nerves?
5. Have you ever dreaded going to a family event because of a personality clash with one of your relatives?
6. What have you enjoyed about family get-togethers?

The results. Over 92 per cent (1,358) of the random individuals who were reached did answer the survey. Here are the actual numbers and percentages for the questions and answers:

2. Do you have any immediate or extended family who get together for holiday meals, birthday meals, or other family events?

   76 per cent (1041) said yes, 23 per cent (317) said no

3. How would you describe your family holiday events and get-togethers?

   a. Enjoyable – 32 per cent (332)

   b. Sometimes enjoyable, but sometimes very difficult – 41 per cent (427)

   c. Rarely enjoyable, but an obligation I do anyway – 27 per cent (282)

   d. We don't get together because of (ranked according to frequency of response): geography, death, tensions, no one takes the initiative

4. Is there someone in your immediate or extended family who gets on your nerves?

   Yes – 77 per cent (913); no – 23 per cent (445)

5. Have you ever dreaded going to a family holiday event because of a personality clash with one of your relatives?

   Yes – 58 per cent (788); no – 42 per cent (570)

6. What have you enjoyed about family holiday get-togethers?

   There was a range of answers, including many who said 'To catch up with family members I miss and love', 'To see the younger ones', 'To spend time with loved ones who are getting older', 'The food', 'The traditions', 'The camaraderie', 'The laughter', 'The sense that we all have something in common', etc.

Conclusions. What does this research mean to you and your family situation? Here are some conclusions that can be drawn from the study:

1. The initial hypothesis or assumption of most people is wrong. It turns out that if you have family conflicts or difficult relatives, you are neither alone nor part of a small percentage of troubled families. In fact, this study reveals for the first time the widespread prevalence of family personality clashes, which are much more prevalent than my colleagues or I expected. Over 75 per cent of us have a relative who gets on our nerves. More than 67 per cent of us find our family get-togethers to be 'sometimes very difficult' or 'an obligation that is rarely enjoyable, but I do it anyway.'

2. A large number of families have ambivalent feelings each year when religious or secular celebrations occur. This study reveals that only 23 per cent of families avoid each other altogether while the vast majority of families get together even though they find the events 'difficult at times' or they are at odds with at least one family member.

3. Most of the respondents, including most of those who said they have difficult relatives or stressful family get-togethers, still had some good things to say about their family gatherings. It seems that even if there are difficult moments, there is still a strong desire to connect with family members at various times during the year.

4. Rather than feeling ashamed or deficient for having a difficult family situation, it seems more accurate according to this study to see yourself as part of the vast majority of men and women who want family closeness but who have to contend with one or more difficult relatives each year.

Future research. I hope there will be more studies in future to clarify or refine these conclusions. Research that helps us understand what goes on in our families and how to respond more effectively to our difficult relatives is long overdue.

SOURCES AND
SUGGESTED READINGS

Chapter One, page 20

'In the past ten years there have been some exciting discoveries by the scientists conducting the human genome project... One of the remarkable findings has been that there seems to be, *by design*, a range and severity of personality diversity among members of the same family.'

This research is summarized in the book *Shadow Syndromes* by John Ratey and Catherine Johnson (New York: Pantheon, 1997) in 'New Brain Science: Is Everybody Crazy?' by Sharon Begley, *Newsweek* magazine, January 26, 1998, pages 50–56, and in 'The Blank Slate: Why Are We Who We Are?' *Discovery* magazine, October 2002, pages 34–40.

Chapter One, page 20

'Genetic research shows that in families there are usually one or two people who are prone to narcissistic tendencies...'

The three sources listed above (*Shadow Syndromes*, *Newsweek* 1/26/98, and *Discovery* 10/02) describe the genetics research on personality disorders. For more on the specific issue of narcissistic family members, see *The Diagnostic and Statistic Manual of Mental Disorders*, Fourth Edition (Washington, D.C.: The American Psychiatric Association, 1994), pages 658–661; *Children of the Self-Absorbed* by Nina Brown (Oakland, Calif.: New Harbinger, 2001); *The Narcissistic Family* by Stephanie Donaldson-Pressman and Robert Pressman (San Francisco: Jossey-Bass, 1997); and *Why Is It Always about You?* by Sandy Hotchkiss (New York: Free Press, 2002).

Chapter One, page 22
'As Reinhold Niebuhr said so eloquently almost eighty years ago....'

He first said the Serenity prayer in his sermons to his congregation and it can be found in *The Essential Reinhold Niebuhr* by Robert McAfee Brown (New York: Yale, 1987).

Chapter Two, page 36
'But scientific studies have taught us since that offloading on someone doesn't actually reduce the level of anger....'

For insights into why venting anger doesn't help either the person doing the venting, the person receiving the venting, or the relationship between the two people, see *Anger, the Misunderstood Emotion* by Carol Tavris (New York: Simon and Schuster, 1989); 'The Expression of Anger and Its Consequences,' by Jerry Deffenbacher, in *Behavior Research and Therapy*, Volume 34, 1996b, pages 575–590; and *Treatment of Patients with Anger-Control Problems and Aggressive Behaviors* by Donald Meichenbaum (Waterloo, Ontario: University of Waterloo, 2001).

Chapter Two, page 55
'...Arnold Beisser developed and studied the effectiveness of something he called *the paradoxical theory of change*....'

This 1970 article can be found on pages 77–80 of an

anthology titled *Gestalt Therapy Now* by Joen Fagan and Irma Shepherd (New York: Harper, 1970).

Chapter Three, page 83

'... the *Challenger* space shuttle...'

For more on the scientific explanations of what happened, see 'Challenger Disaster,' *Microsoft Encarta Online Encyclopedia 2002*.

Chapter Four, page 106

'Is there a book, an activity or a one-off event that you would be willing to experience with an open mind....'

In addition to whatever you and your family member choose for the other person to experience and understand about your different spiritual paths, there is also an excellent series of books written for people who want to be respectful and compassionate toward the religious and spiritual practices of others. The books are titled *How to Be a Perfect Stranger: A Guide to Etiquette in Other People's Religious Ceremonies*, by Stuart Matlins and Arthur Magida (Woodstock, Vt.: SkyLight Paths, 1999).

Chapter Seven, page 155

'. . . a black-and-white version of the classic film *Dr Jekyll and Mr Hyde . . .*' refers to the 1932 Oscar-winning film with Frederic March, directed by Rouben Mamoulian, from the story by Robert Louis Stevenson.

Chapter Eight, page 189

'... a series of religious papers, articles, and speeches put together by Rabbi Elliott Dorff....'

For more on the debate within Conservative Judaism about gay and lesbian equality, see 'Out of the Closet: Will the Conservative Movement Reopen the Issue of Gay Rabbis?' by Julie Gruenbaum Fax, *The Jewish Journal of Greater Los Angeles*, Volume 17, Number 47, January 17–23, 2003, pages 12–13; and *Love Your Neighbor and Yourself: A Jewish Approach to Modern Personal Ethics*, by Elliott Dorff (Philadelphia: Jewish Publication Society, 2003).

Chapter Eight, page 191
The Biblical passage 'And the truth shall set you free' is from John 8:32.

Chapter Eight, page 193
'… three different written viewpoints on the issue….'

I urge you to ask for various viewpoints from your own minister, priest, or rabbi to find out about debates and differing views within your particular denomination. In addition, you can find various viewpoints on religion and homosexuality in *What the Bible Really Says about Homosexuality*, by Daniel A. Helminiak (a Roman Catholic priest) (San Francisco: Alamo Square Press, 2000); *Openly Gay, Openly Christian*, by Samuel Kader (a Protestant minister) (San Francisco: Leyland Publications, 1999); *Welcoming but Not Affirming*, by Stanley J. Grenz (an Evangelical minister) (Louisville: Westminster John Knox Press, 1998); and *Lesbian Rabbis: The First Generation*, by Rebecca T. Alpert, Sue Levi Elwell, and Shirley Idelson (a Reconstructionist rabbi and two Reform rabbis) (Piscataway, N.J.: Rutgers University Press, 2001).

RESOURCES

GENERAL
UNITED KINGDOM
Relate
www.relate.org.uk
Tel: 0845 130 4010
Relate offer advice, relationship counselling and support in person, over the phone and online.

AUSTRALIA
Relationships Australia
www.relationships.com.au
www.relationshipshelponline.com.au
Tel: 1300 364 277
Relationships Australia offer resources and services, including counselling and mediation, for couples, individuals and families.

NEW ZEALAND
Relationship Services
www.relate.org.nz
This not-for-profit organization provides counselling and education services for families and individuals.

SOUTH AFRICA
Family and Marriage Association of South Africa (FAMSA)
www.famsa.org.za
Tel: 011 975 7106/ 082 231 0380
FAMSA is a not-for-profit organization that offers counselling for families, couples and individuals, as well as projects in community development and training.

ALCOHOL

UNITED KINGDOM
AL-ANON Family Groups UK and Eire
www.al-anonuk.org.uk
Tel: 020 7403 0888 (24 hr helpline)
Fax: 020 7378 9910
Al-Anon aims to help families and friends of alcoholics recover from the effects of living with a problem drinker.

Alateen
www.hexnet.co.uk/alanon/alateen.html
Tel: 020 7403 0888 (24 hr helpline)
Fax: 020 7378 9910
Alateen is part of the Al-Anon fellowship and is for young people, aged 12–20, who are affected by a problem drinker.

Alcoholics Anonymous
www.alcoholics-anonymous.org.uk
Tel: 0845 769 7555 (24 hr helpline)
The UK branch of Alcoholics Anonymous. The only requirement for AA membership is a desire to stop drinking. There are no fees.

Drinkline – The National Alcohol Helpline
Tel: 0800 917 8282 (24 hr helpline)

National Association of Children of Alcoholics
www.nacoa.org.uk
Tel: 0800 289061

AUSTRALIA
Alcoholics Anonoymous, Australia
www.aa.org.au

NEW ZEALAND
Alcoholics Anonymous, NZ
www.alcoholics-anonymous.org.nz

Ministry of Health Alcohol Helpline
Tel: 0800 787 797

SOUTH AFRICA
Alcoholics Anonymous, SA
www.alcoholicsanonymous.cape.org.za

DRUGS

UNITED KINGDOM
BBC One Life: Drugs
www.bbc.co.uk/radio1/onelife/health/index.shtml?drugs#topics
Information on drugs as well as links to support
organizations.

Council for Involuntary Tranquilliser Addiction (CITA)
Tel: 0151 474 9636 (24 hr helpline)
Information and support for people addicted to prescription
tranquillizers.

Families Anonymous
www.famanon.org.uk
Tel: 0845 1200 660
Families Anonymous is a support organization for the families of drug abusers. The organization is based on the twelve-step programme.

Talk to Frank
www.talktofrank.com
Tel: 0800 776600 (24 hr helpline)
An anonymous, discreet and well-informed friend – Frank is on the phone or the web to talk to young people, parents and carers worried about drugs.

Australia
Drug-Arm (Drug Awareness Rehabilitation and Management)
www.drugarm.com.au
Tel: 1300 656 800
Information, support and advice for drug users, their families and friends as well as the wider community.

Australian Drug Foundation (ADF)
www.adf.org.au
Tel: (03) 9278 8100
An independent, non-profit organization aiming to reduce drug and alcohol-related problems in the Australian community.

New Zealand
Alcohol and Drug Association, New Zealand
www.adanz.org.nz
Tel: 0800 787 797 (Alcohol and drug helpline)
Not-for-profit community organization that offers a range of

information on drugs and alcohol, including a support programme for parents.

SOUTH AFRICA
Narcotics Anonymous
www.na.org.za
Tel: Gauteng: 011 48 552 48
Western Cape: 088 130 0327
KwaZulu-Natal: 088 127 8832
(meeting enquiries: 088 124 6436)

GAY AND LESBIAN

UNITED KINGDOM
FFLAG (Families and Friends of Lesbians and Gays)
www.fflag.org.uk
Tel: 01454 852 418 (Helpline)
FFLAG is a national registered charity offering support to families and friends of lesbians and gays. They operate helplines across the UK and also run parents' groups.

AUSTRALIA
PFLAG (Parents, Families and Friends of Lesbians and Gays)
www.pflagaustralia.org
Australian chapter of this international support organization. PFLAG has branches in most major Australian cities.

NEW ZEALAND
PFLAG South/ PFLAG Wellington (Parents and Friends of Lesbians and Gays)
au.geocities.com/pflagsouth
New Zealand chapters of this international organization.

SOUTH AFRICA
See FAMSA, p. 248

PFLAG Overport-Durban
Overport Durban
South Africa 4067

ABUSE

UNITED KINGDOM
NSPCC
www.nspcc.org.uk
Tel: 0808 800 5000 (24 hr helpline)
E-mail: help@nspcc.org.uk
Textphone (for people who are deaf or hearing impaired):
0800 056 0566
The NSPCC provide resources relating to child safety and
advice for parents, carers and children.
See also:
www.there4me.com
A confidential online advice service for teenagers run by the
NSPCC.

BBC Hitting Home campaign
www.bbc.co.uk/health/hh
Information, help and support for anyone affected by
domestic violence.

Women's Aid
www.womensaid.org.uk
Tel: 08457 023 468 (24 hr domestic violence helpline)
Women's Aid offers support and refuge for women and
children affected by domestic violence.

Home Office Domestic Violence leaflet
www.homeoffice.gov.uk/docs3/domestic_violence_a5_eng.pdf
(requires Adobe Acrobat Reader)
This leaflet offers advice and information for people
experiencing domestic violence, their friends and family.

Refuge
Tel: 0990 995 443 (24 hr national crisis line)

Men's Advice Line
Tel: 020 8644 9914

AUSTRALIA
National Association for Prevention of Child Abuse and Neglect (NAPCAN)
www.napcan.org.au
An independent charity committed to stopping child abuse,
NAPCAN provides information and resources for children,
families and the community on child safety and protection.

Kids Helpline
www.kidshelp.com.au
Tel: 1800 551800 (24 hr helpline)
National 24-hour telephone and online counselling service
for children and young people in Australia.

Partnership Against Domestic Violence
www.padv.dpmc.gov.au
This commonwealth government initiative works with state
governments and community organizations to prevent
domestic violence. Their website includes information
about domestic violence in Australia, and provides a list of
organizations that work to prevent domestic violence,
including organizations that provide emergency assistance.

Broken Rites
brokenrites.alphalink.com.au
Tel: (03) 9457 4999
Broken Rites is a non-denominational support group for people who have been abused sexually, physically or emotionally in religious institutions. Broken Rites offers support and advocacy for victims.

New Zealand
Parentline
www.parentline.org.nz
Parentline is an advocacy service for children who have been sexually, physically or emotionally abused or who are at risk of abuse. They offer counselling and support programmes for children and families.

Youthline
www.youthline.co.nz
Tel: 0800 376 633
Youthline provides confidential support for young people throughout NZ/Aotearoa.

National Network of Stopping Violence Services
Tel: 04 499 6384
Fax: 04 499 6387
Email: *nnsvs@freemail.co.nz*

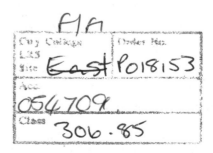

SOUTH AFRICA
Childline South Africa
Tel: 0800 055 555 (24 hr helpline)
Childline is a not-for profit organization providing
assistance from trained counsellors for abused children,
young people and their families.

**Electronic Directory of Services Addressing Gender-
based Violence**
www.csvr.org.za/gender/directory/index.html
This directory provides contact details for organizations
throughout South Africa that work in the area of gender-
based violence, including domestic violence.

Stop Women Abuse, SA
Tel: 0800 150 150

Halt Elder Abuse Line (HEAL)
Tel: 0800 003 081 (office hours only).

OTHER RODALE BOOKS
AVAILABLE FROM PAN MACMILLAN

1-4050-2100-4	The Anorexia Diaries	*Tara Rio and Linda Rio*	£8.99
1-4050-6718-7	Healing Without Freud or Prozac	*Dr David Servan–Schreiber*	£12.99
1-4050-7732-8	How to Help Your Overweight Child	*Karen Sullivan*	£12.99
1-4050-0671-4	Laying Down the Law	*Dr Ruth Peters*	£8.99
1-4050-6719-5	Reclaiming Desire	*Dr Andrew Goldstein and Dr Marianne Branden*	£12.99
1-4050-4728-4	The Secret Life of the Dyslexic Child	*Robert Frank with Kathryn Livingston*	£10.99
1-4050-6728-4	The Shy Single	*Bonnie Jacobson with Sandra J. Gordon*	£10.99
1-4050-3340-1	When Your Body Gets the Blues	*Marie-Annette Brown and Jo Robinson*	£10.99

All Pan Macmillan titles can be ordered from our website, *www.panmacmillan.com,* or from your local bookshop and are also available by post from:

Bookpost, PO Box 29, Douglas, Isle of Man IM99 1BQ
Tel: 01624 836000; fax: 01624 670923; e-mail: *bookshop@enterprise.net*;
or visit: *www.bookpost.co.uk.* Credit cards accepted. Free postage and packing in the United Kingdom

Prices shown above were correct at time of going to press.
Pan Macmillan reserve the right to show new retail prices on covers which may differ from those previously advertised in the text or elsewhere.

For information about buying *Rodale* titles in **Australia**, contact Pan Macmillan Australia.
Tel: 1300 135 113; fax: 1300 135 103; e-mail: *customer.service@macmillan.com.au*;
or visit: *www.panmacmillan.com.au*

For information about buying *Rodale* titles in **New Zealand**, contact Macmillan Publishers
New Zealand Limited. Tel: (09) 414 0356; fax: (09) 414 0352; e-mail: *lyn@macmillan.co.nz*;
or visit: *www.macmillan.co.nz*

For information about buying *Rodale* titles in **South Africa**, contact Pan Macmillan South Africa. Tel: (011) 325 5220; fax: (011) 325 5225; e-mail: *roshni@panmacmillan.co.za*